Michael Sweet's Coney Island

Photographs
Michael Ernest Sweet

Michael Sweet's Coney Island

Photographs
Michael Ernest Sweet

Brooklyn Arts Press
New York

Michael Sweet's Coney Island

ISBN-13: 978-1-936767-40-3

Foreword by Bruce LaBruce

Book design by Joe Pan.
Author photo by Maeghan Donohue.

Published in the United States of America by:
Brooklyn Arts Press, LLC
154 N 9th Street #1
Brooklyn, NY 11249
www.BrooklynArtsPress.com
info@brooklynartspress.com

Library of Congress Control Number: 2014958904

FIRST EDITION

Foreword

by Bruce LaBruce

The digital revolution has changed photography forever. As tempting as it is to regard it as an egalitarian, popular revolution of the form, the democratization of the photographic image, with its casual emphasis on verisimilitude and documentation, runs the risk of erasing classical distinctions of authorship and craft to the point of diminishing the role of the artist altogether. Not everyone is an artist, nor should everyone aspire to be one. Not everyone "has an eye," as the classic synecdoche has it, and not everyone has the sensitivity or intuitiveness, or perhaps even the perverse will and intention, to pursue a pure vision as an artist or photographer. So when someone like Michael Ernest Sweet makes a visual statement of such admirable consistency and acute perverseness, attention must be paid.

With these Coney Island photographs, Mr. Sweet pursues a relentless project of lurid colour, composition, and perspective. Shot with a Japanese Harinezumi toy camera-digital, yes, but with a simple plastic lens producing a more analogue effect-the photographic world he creates suggests a kind of apocalyptic, colour-drenched Weegee capturing the last gasps of a doomed culture. Bloated bodies with electric, pre-cancerous sunburns splayed on the sand invoke not the beaches of the past-the kitschy hopefulness of the fifties; the sexual sultriness of the seventies-but the End of Days lethargy and capitulation of the new millennium. Towel-covered faces and scorched, inert limbs suggest killing fields more than people in the pursuit of pleasure or leisure. A photograph of a man facedown with bruised and bloody knuckles further illustrates, with a latent narrative punch, this impression of bodies beaten and discarded. It's a disturbing landscape, and a fittingly contemporary one.

The Harinezumi camera, with its gaudy saturation of blues and reds, its woozy, distorted, flattened perspective, effectively renders this vision in graphic, abstract realist terms. The photographer's strong sense of composition, itself cutting off limbs or heads, sometimes in favour of banal inanimate objects, completes the effect.

Fittingly, the photographer's shadow seems occasionally to intrude upon the subject of the photograph, a stark reminder of the "eye" of the artist shaping the image and presenting a particularly disturbing, and decidedly post-romantic, portrait of Coney Island, Brooklyn, a paradise lost, a beach at the end of time.

Bruce LaBruce

Toronto, 2014

Michael Sweet's Coney Island

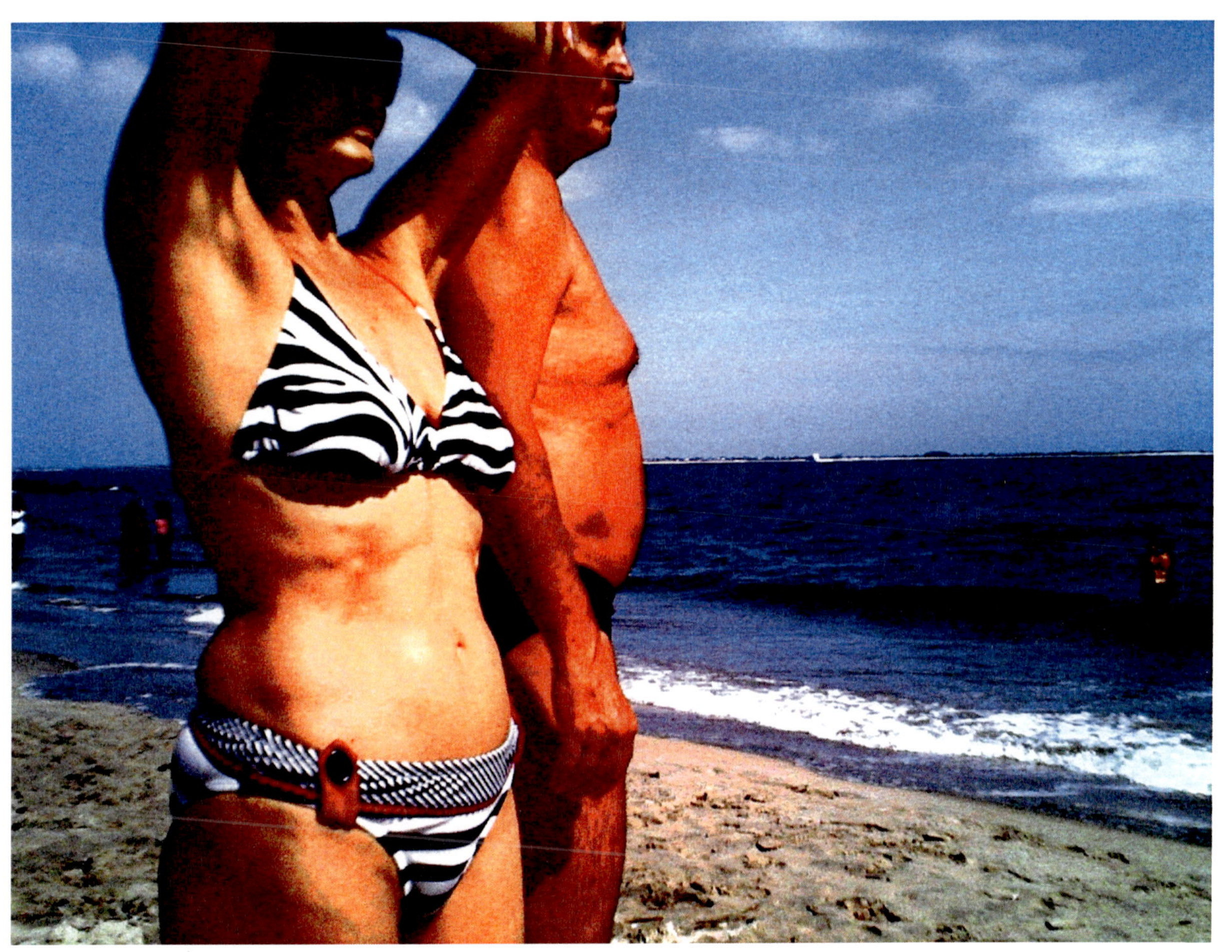

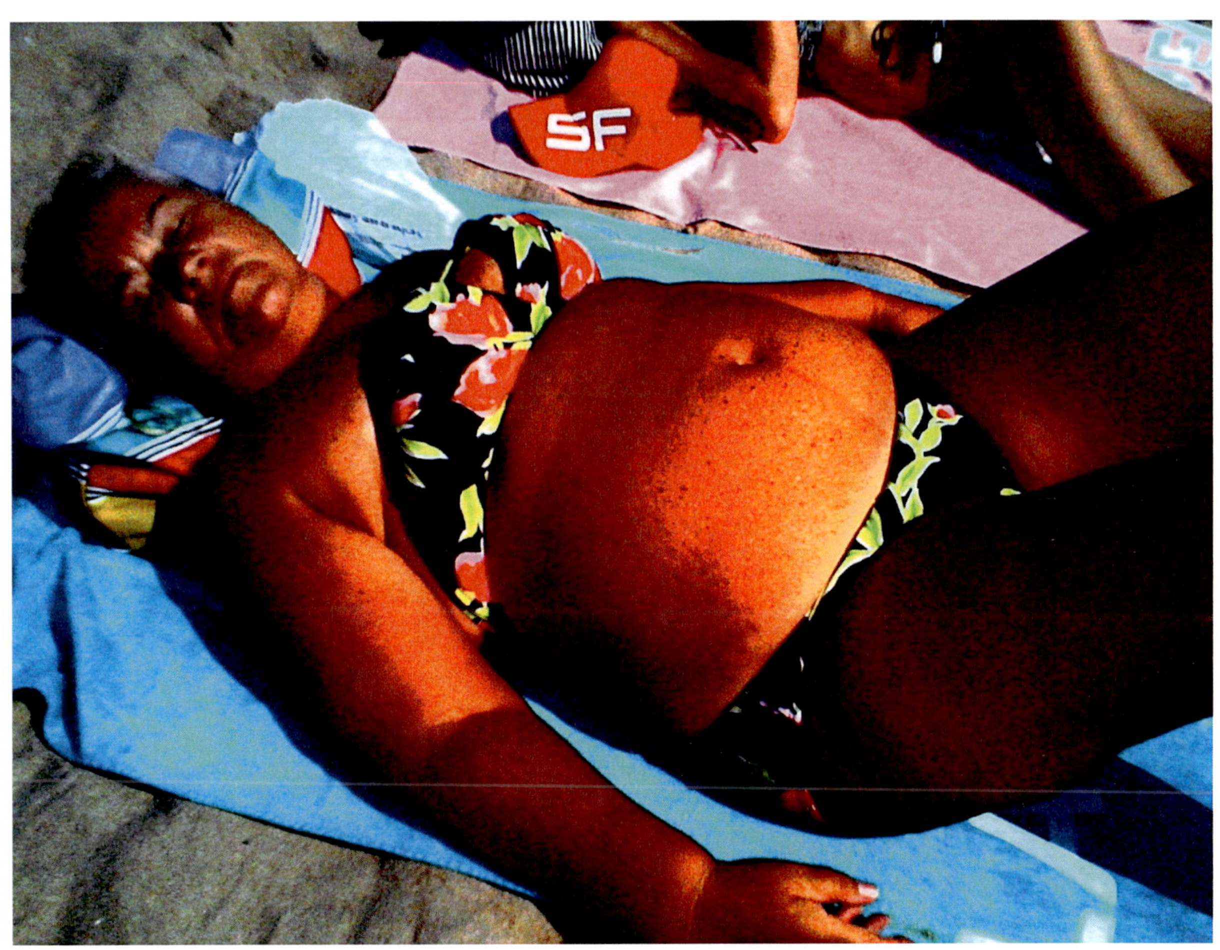
SF

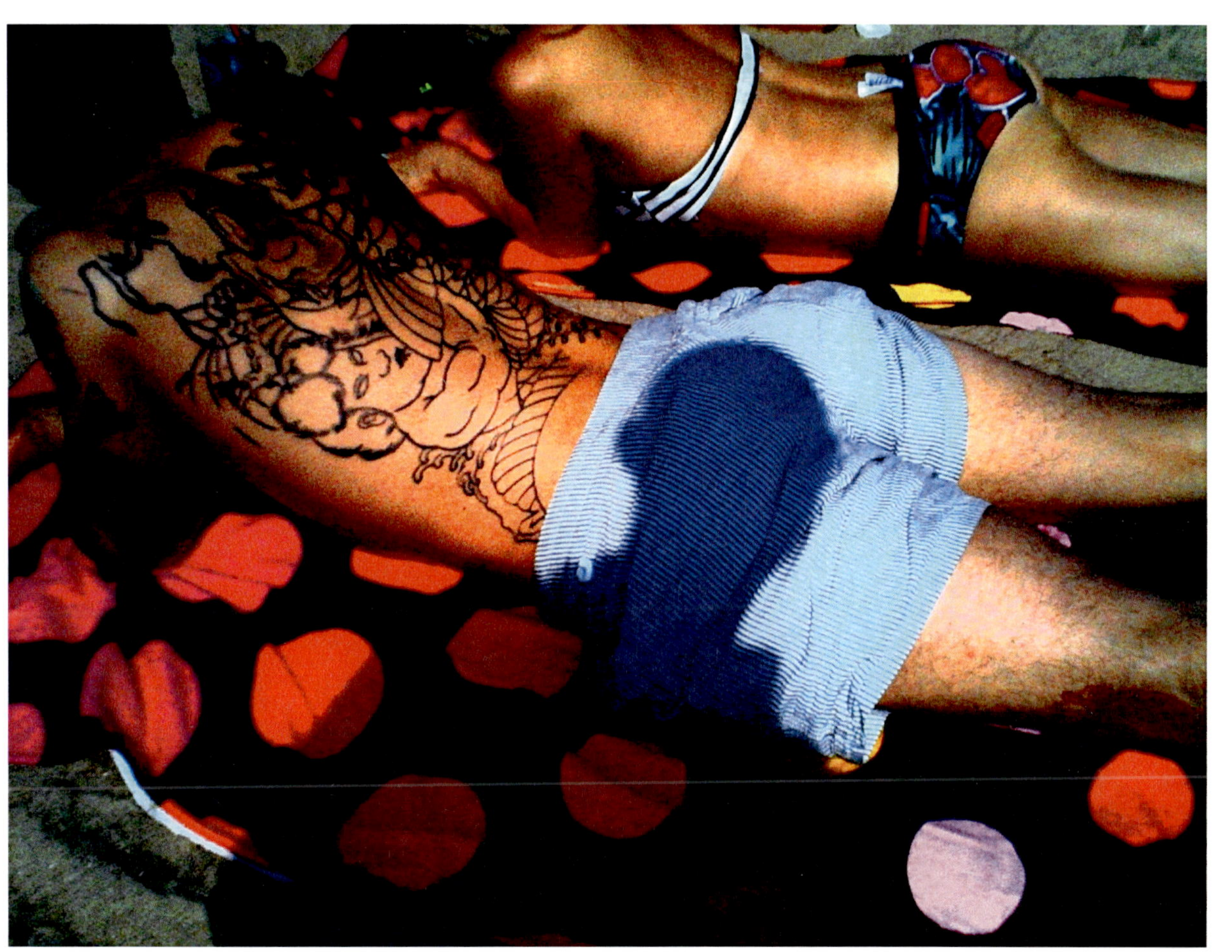

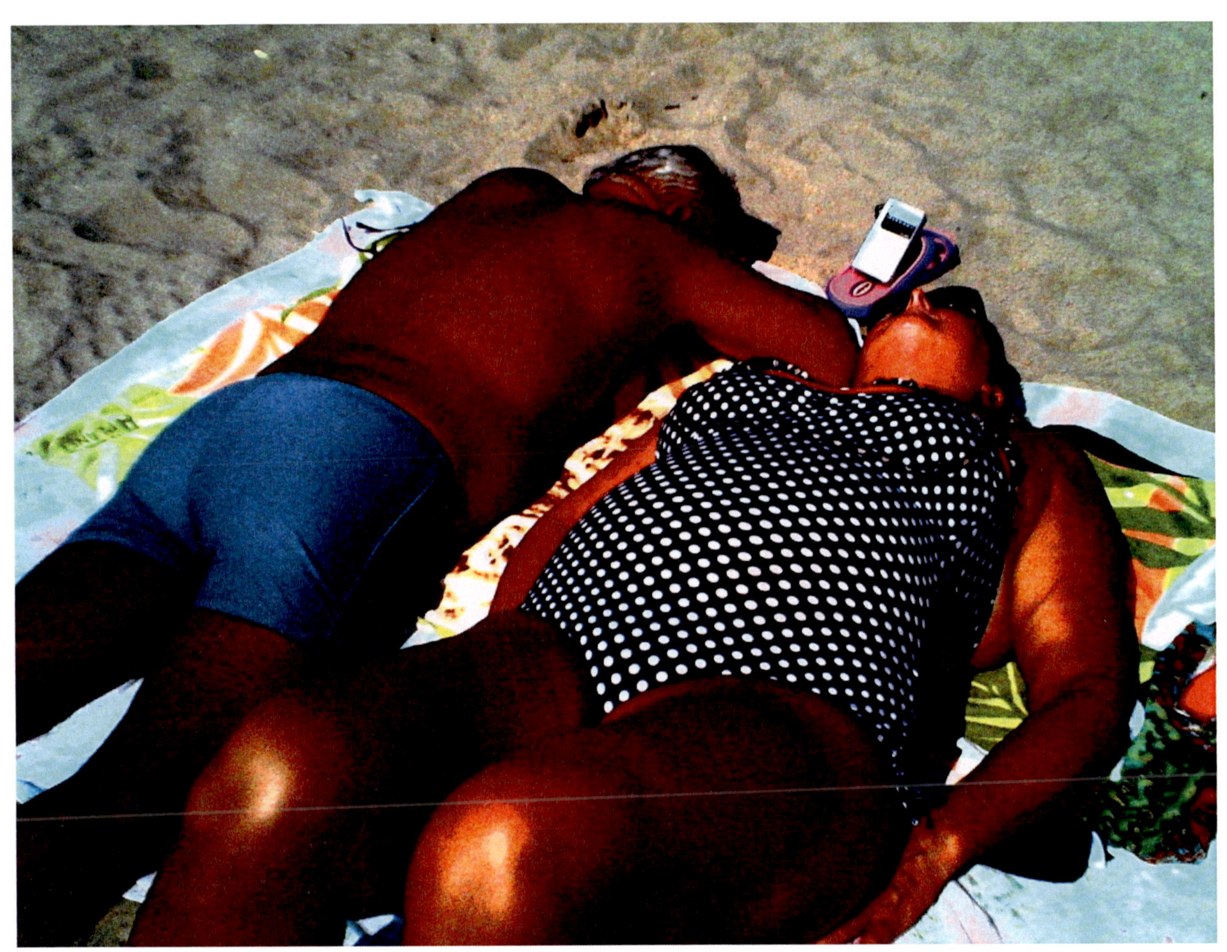

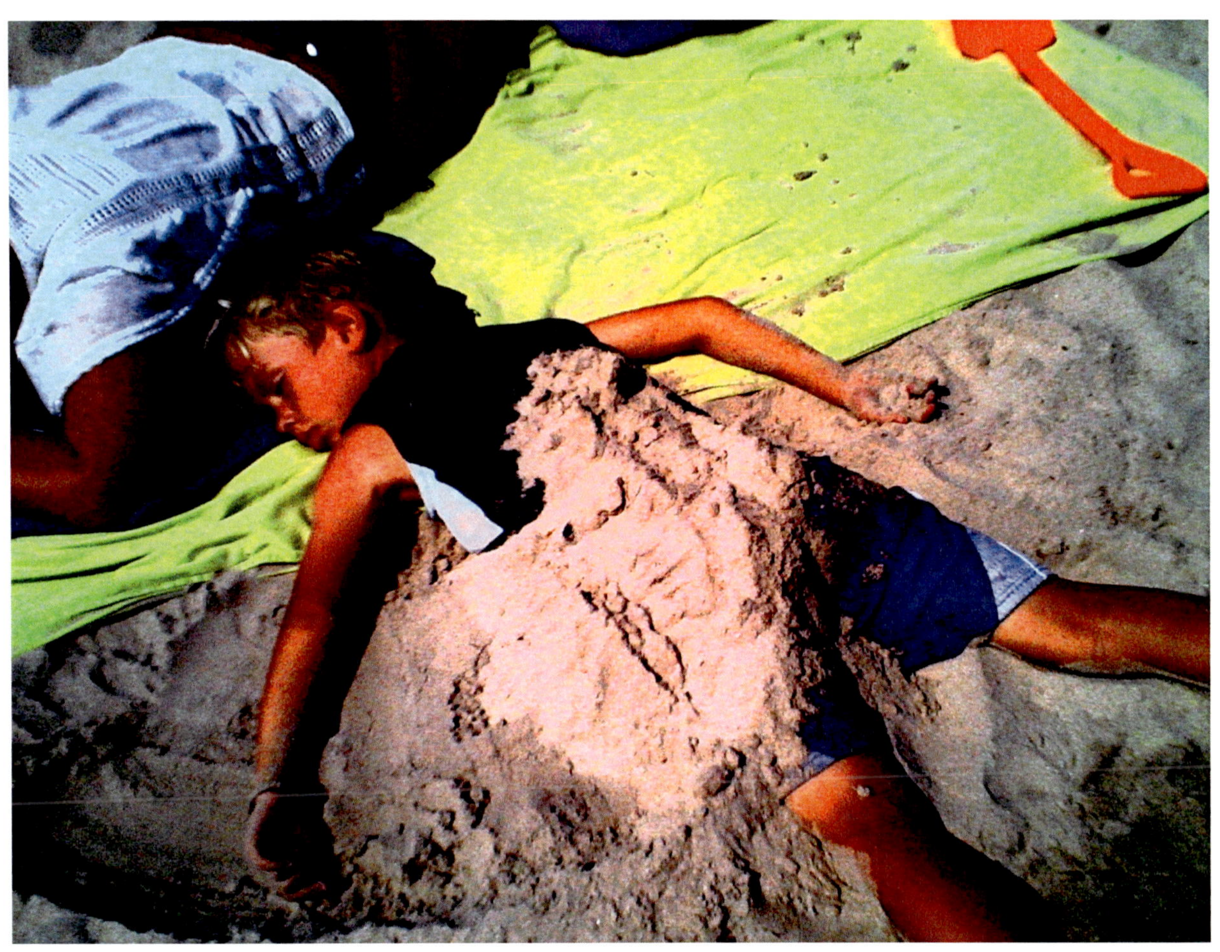

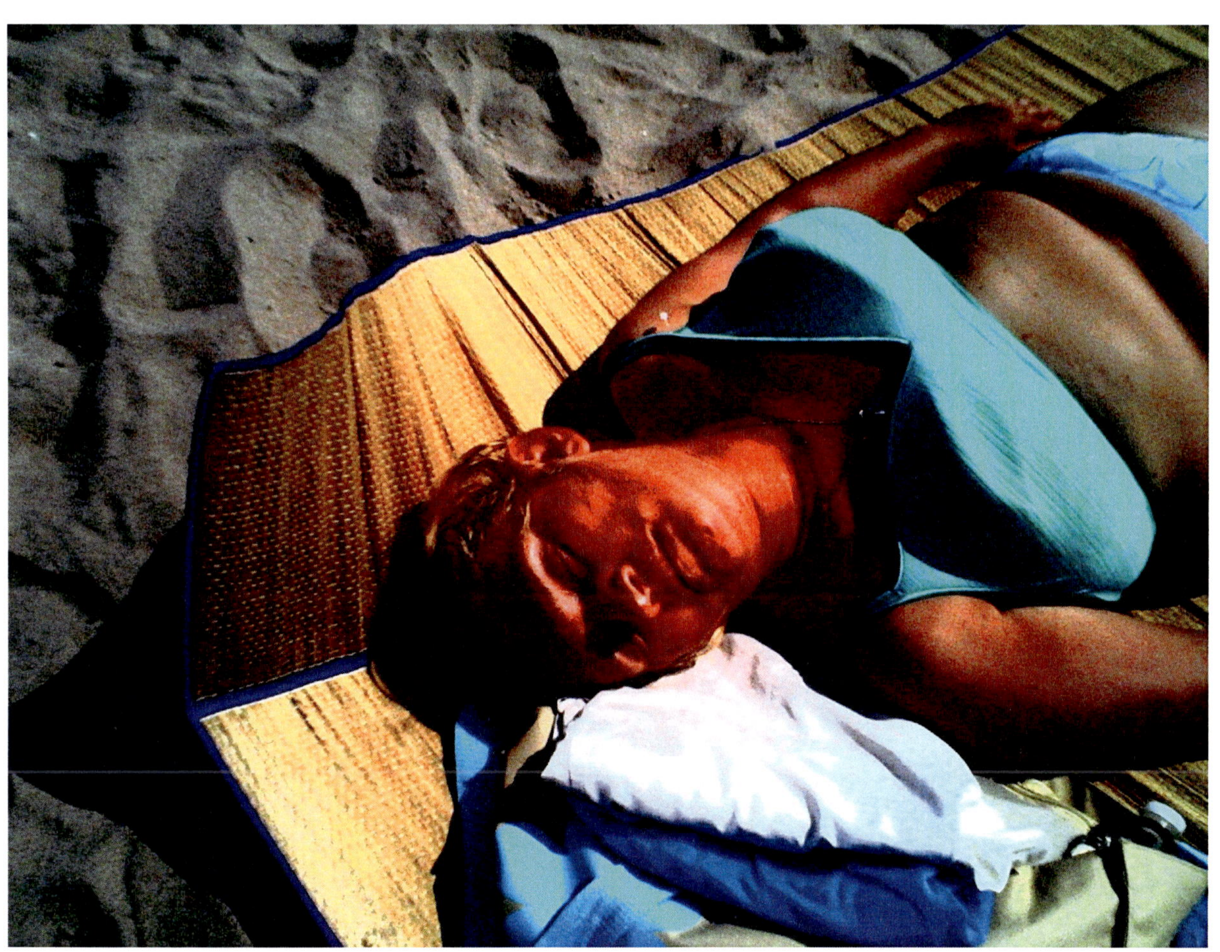

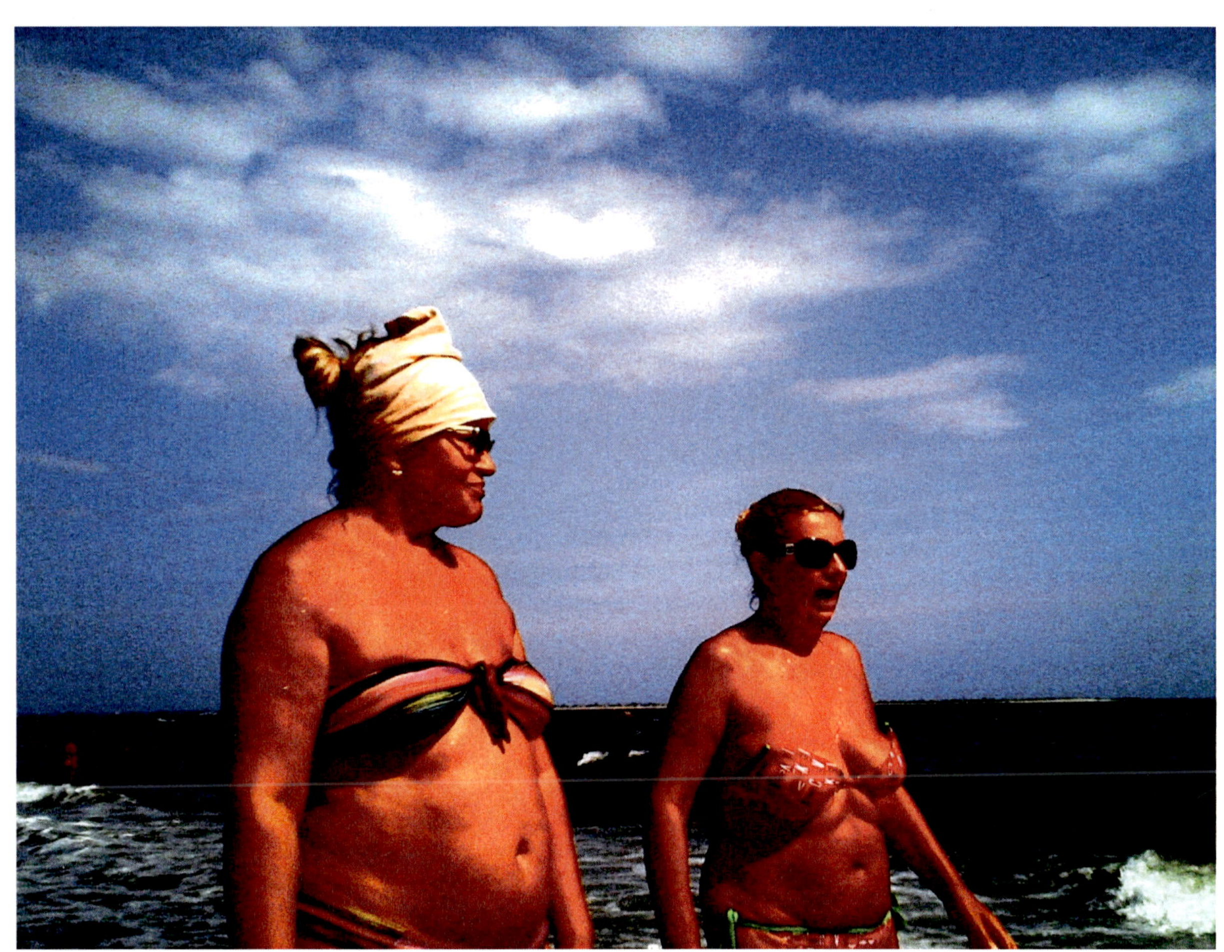

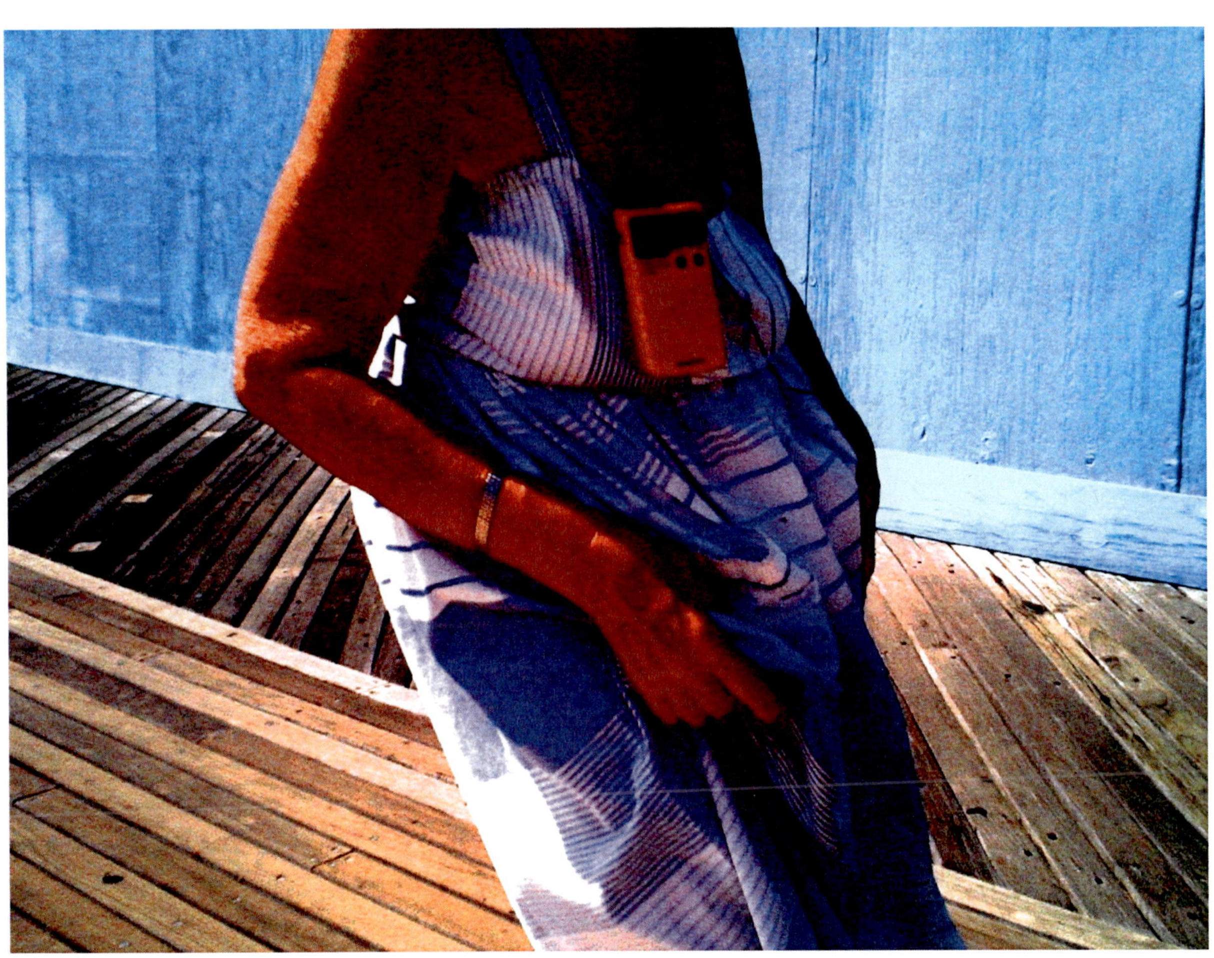

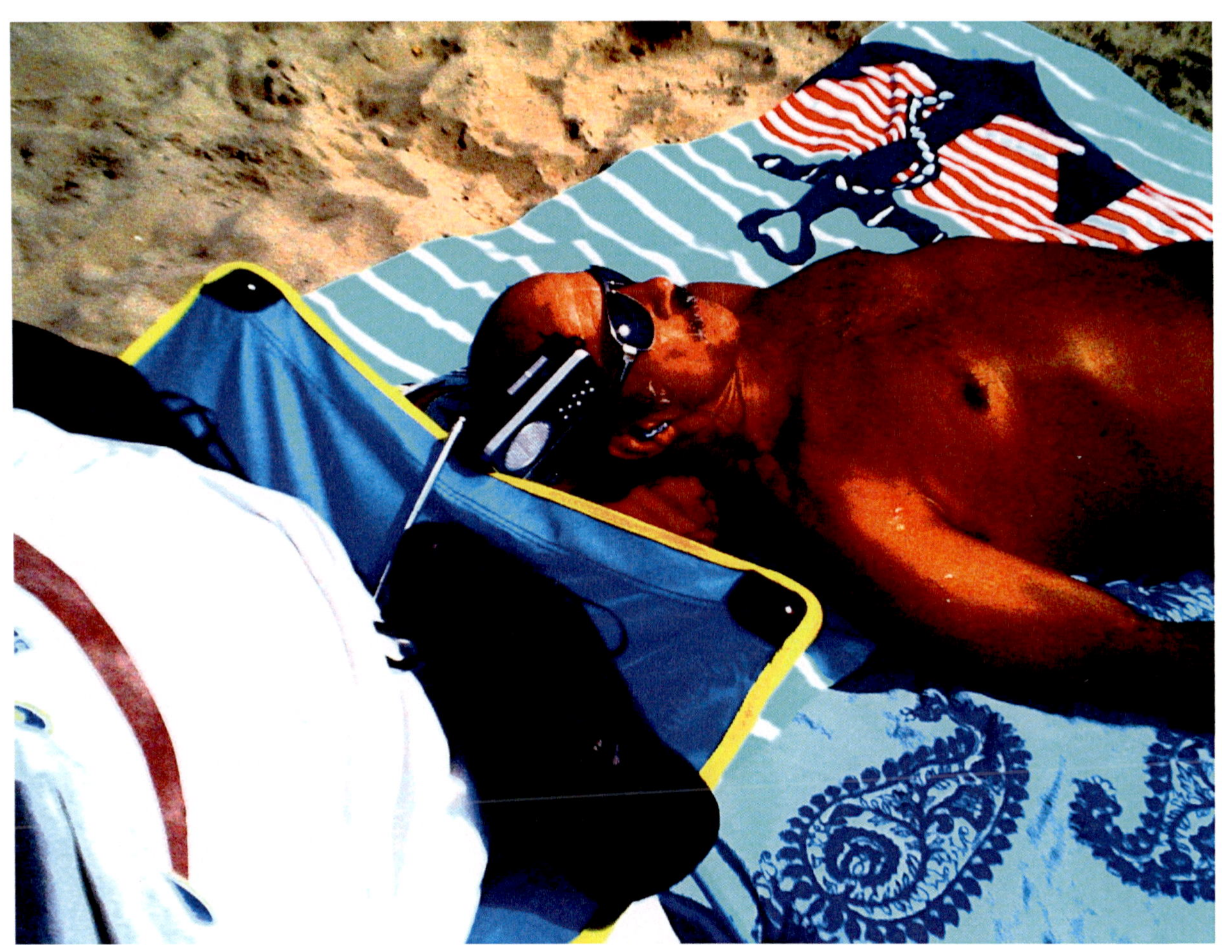

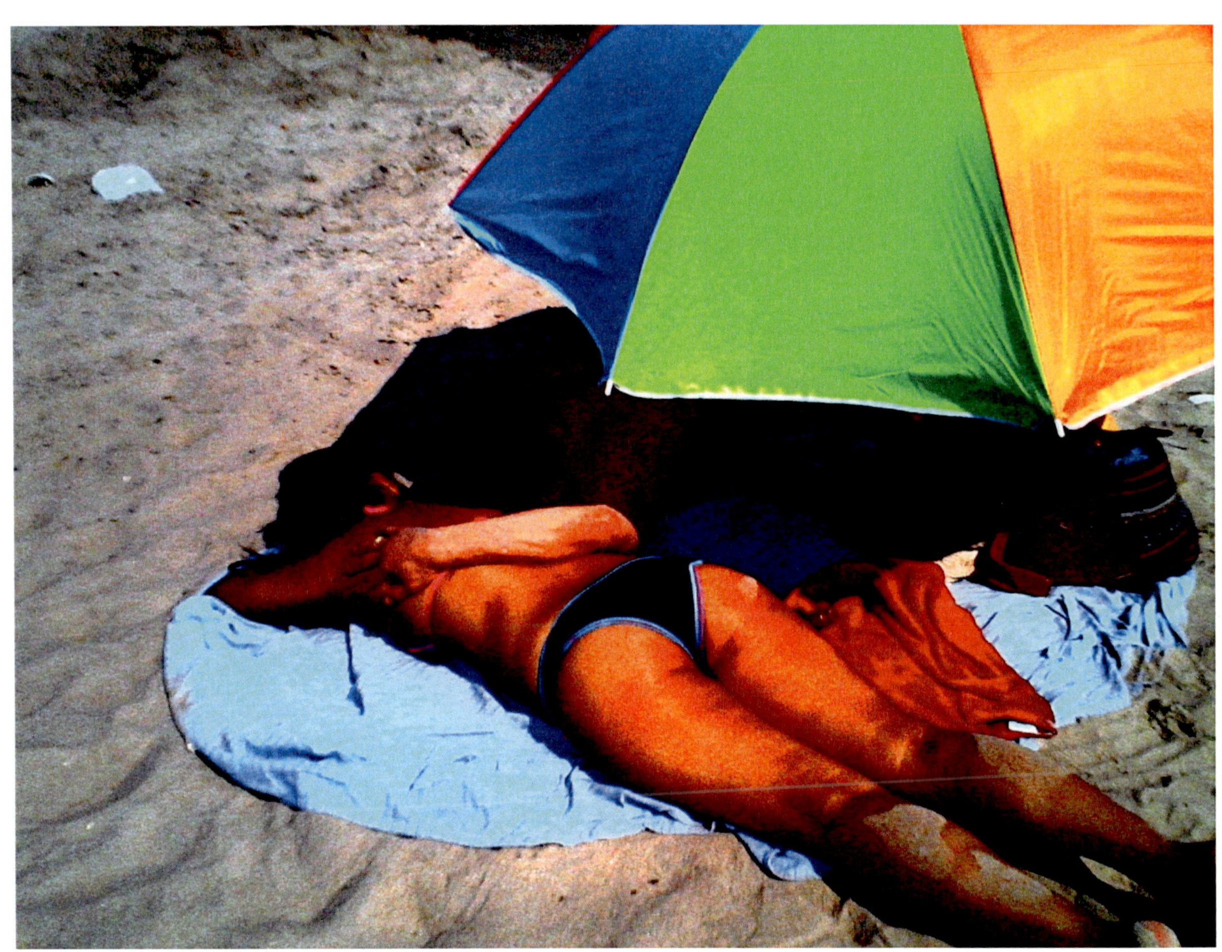

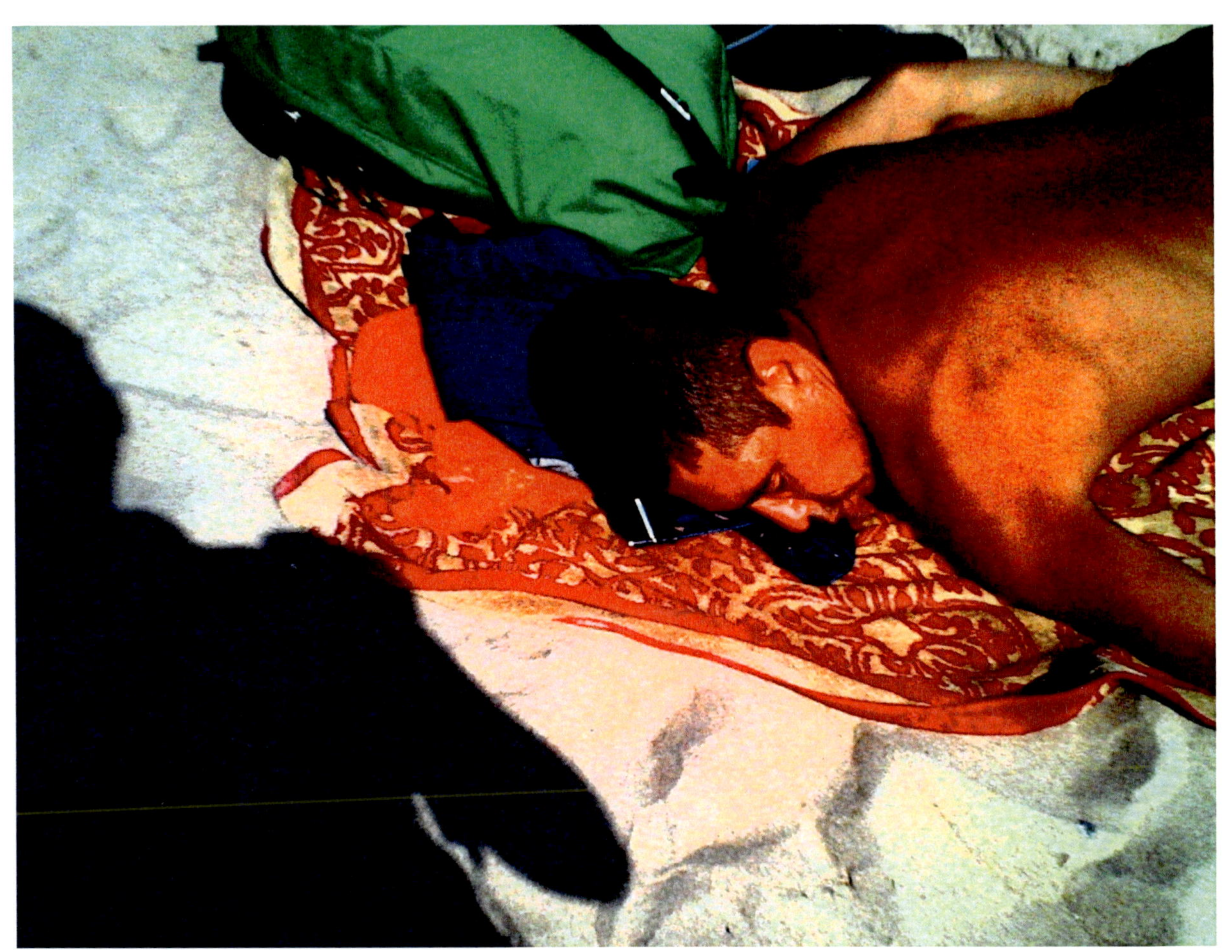

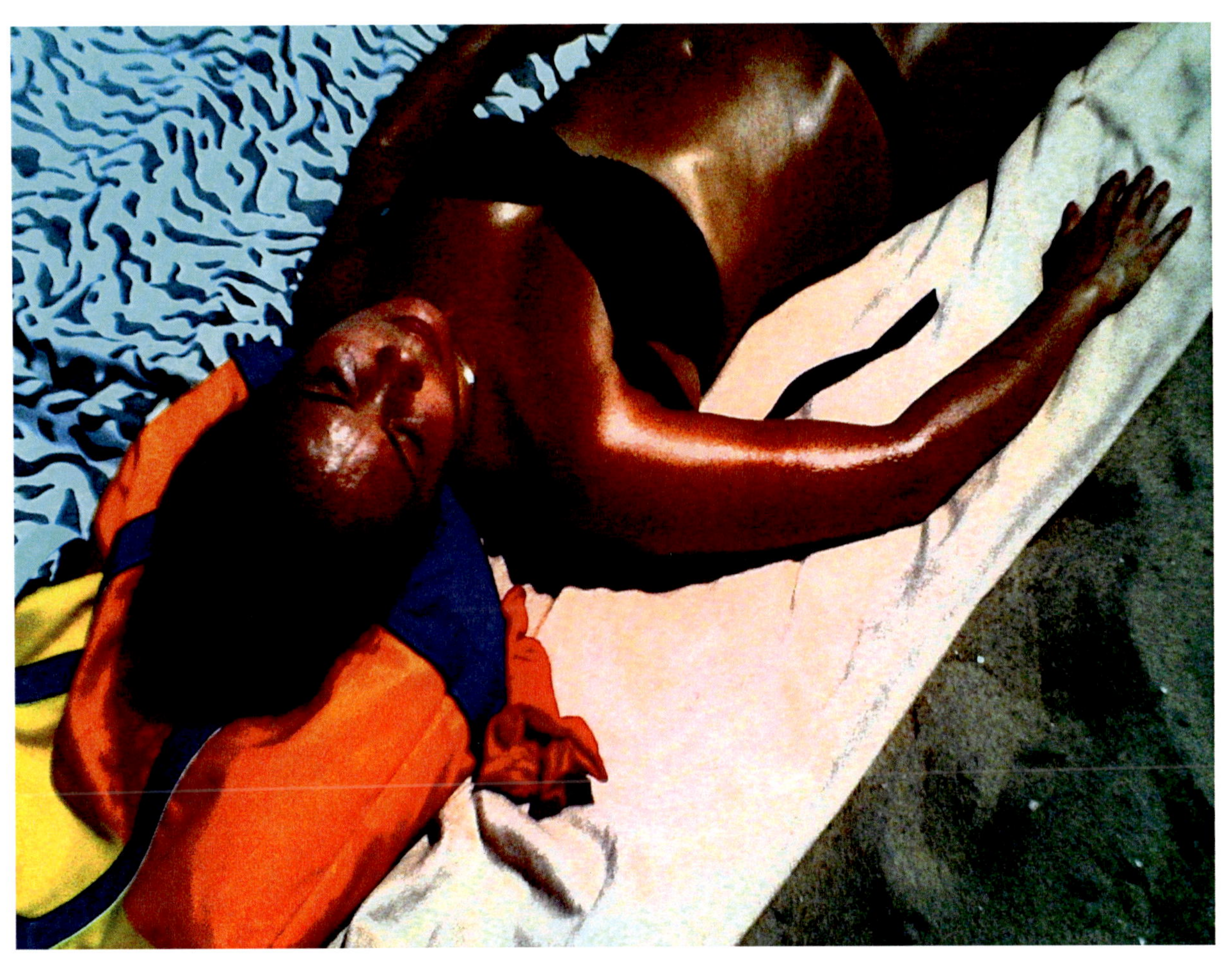

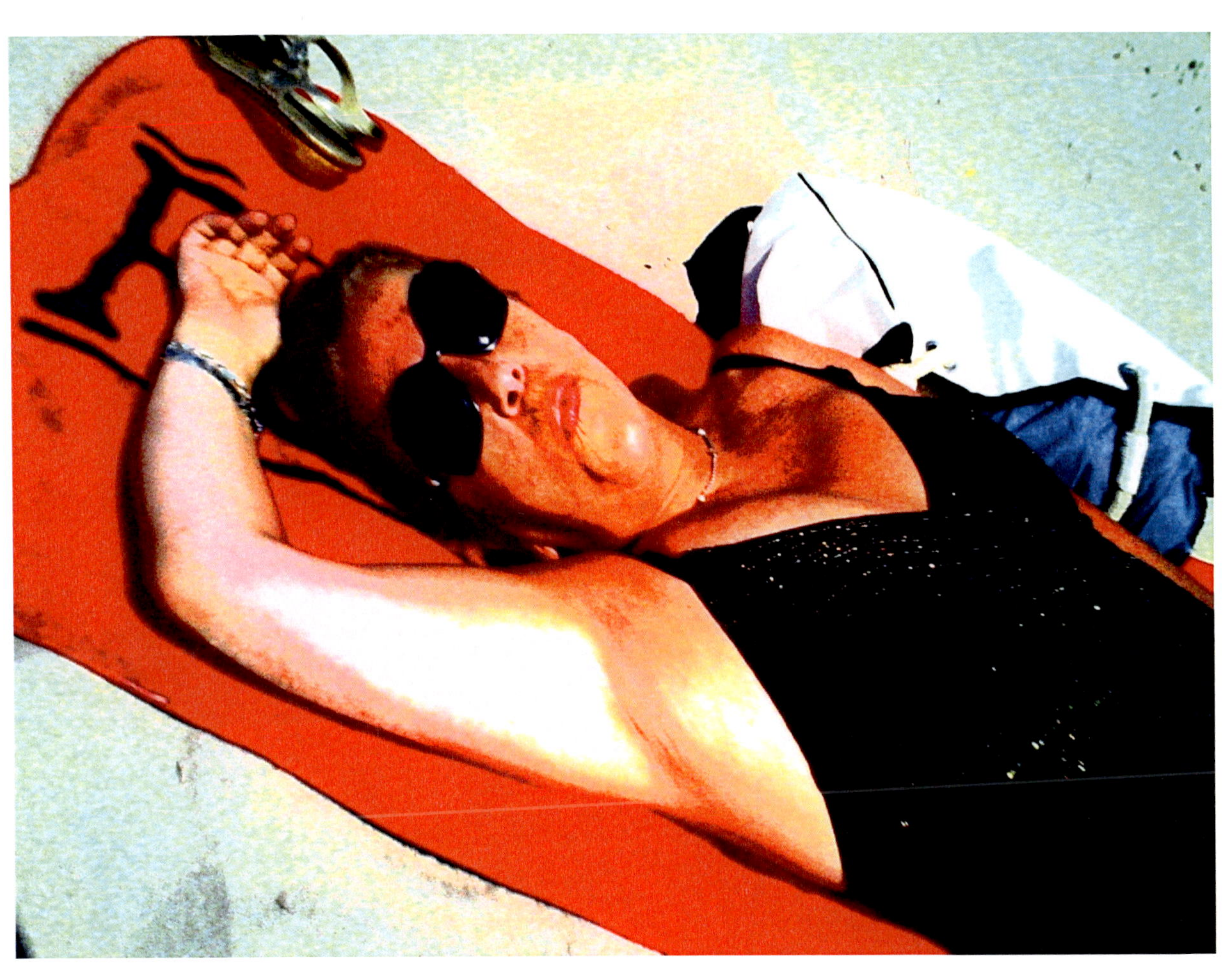

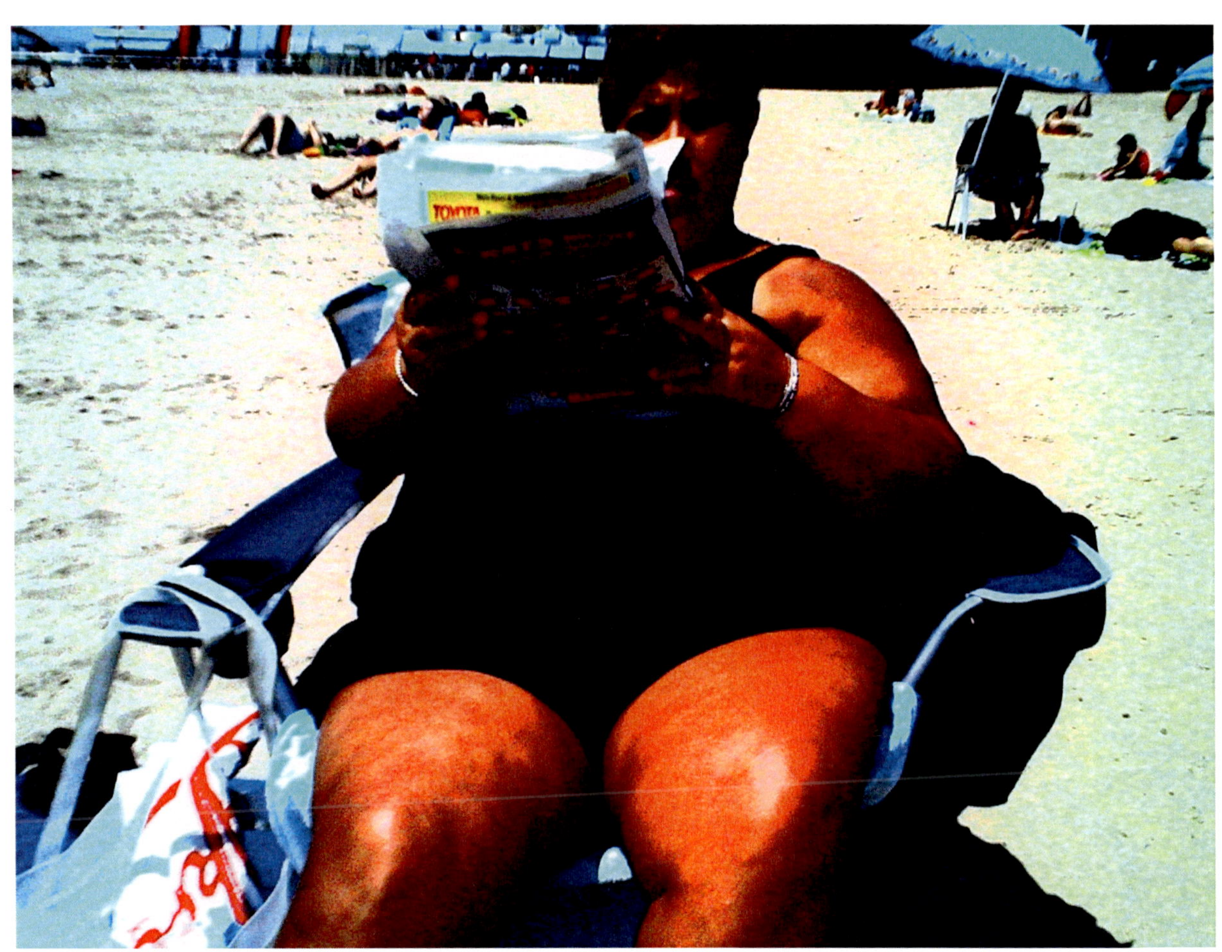

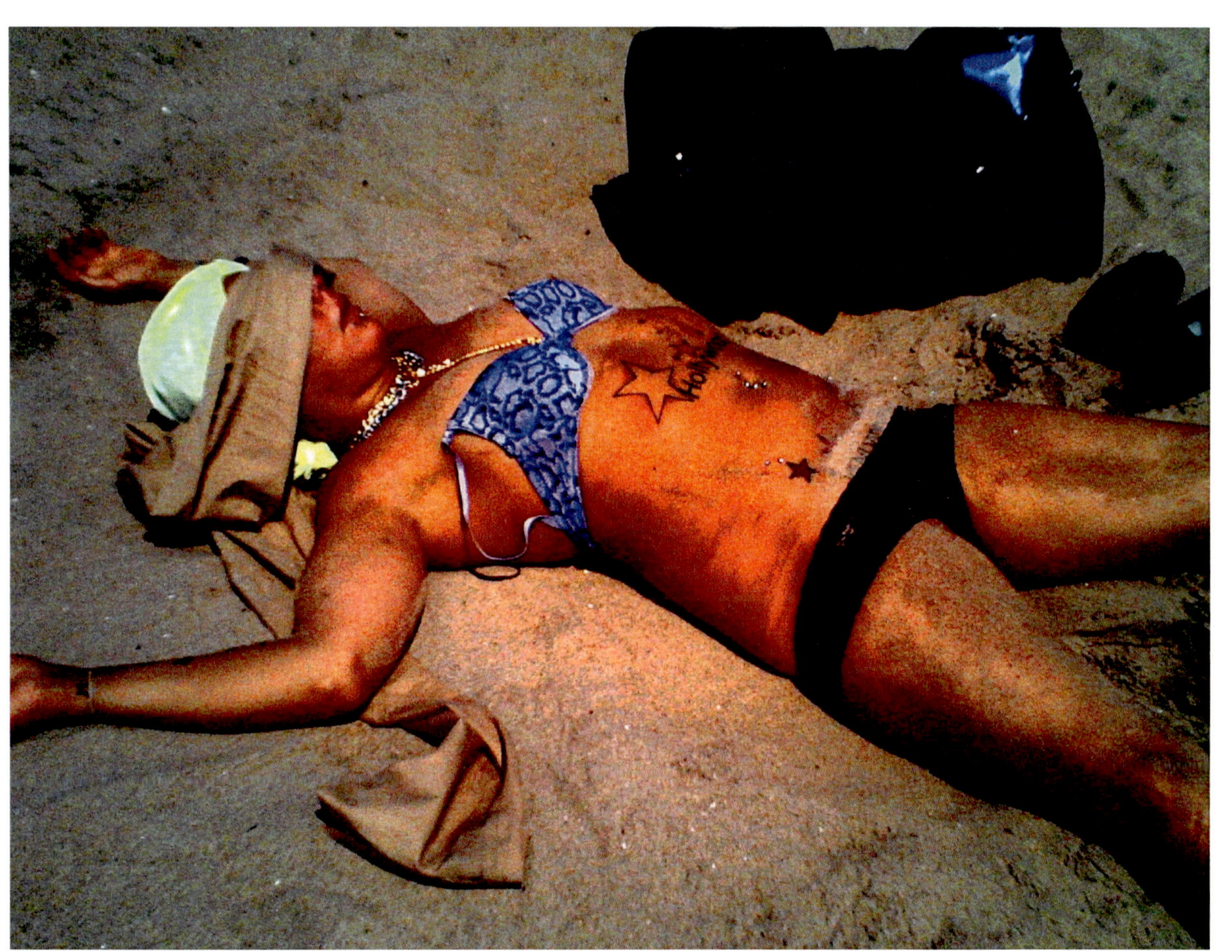

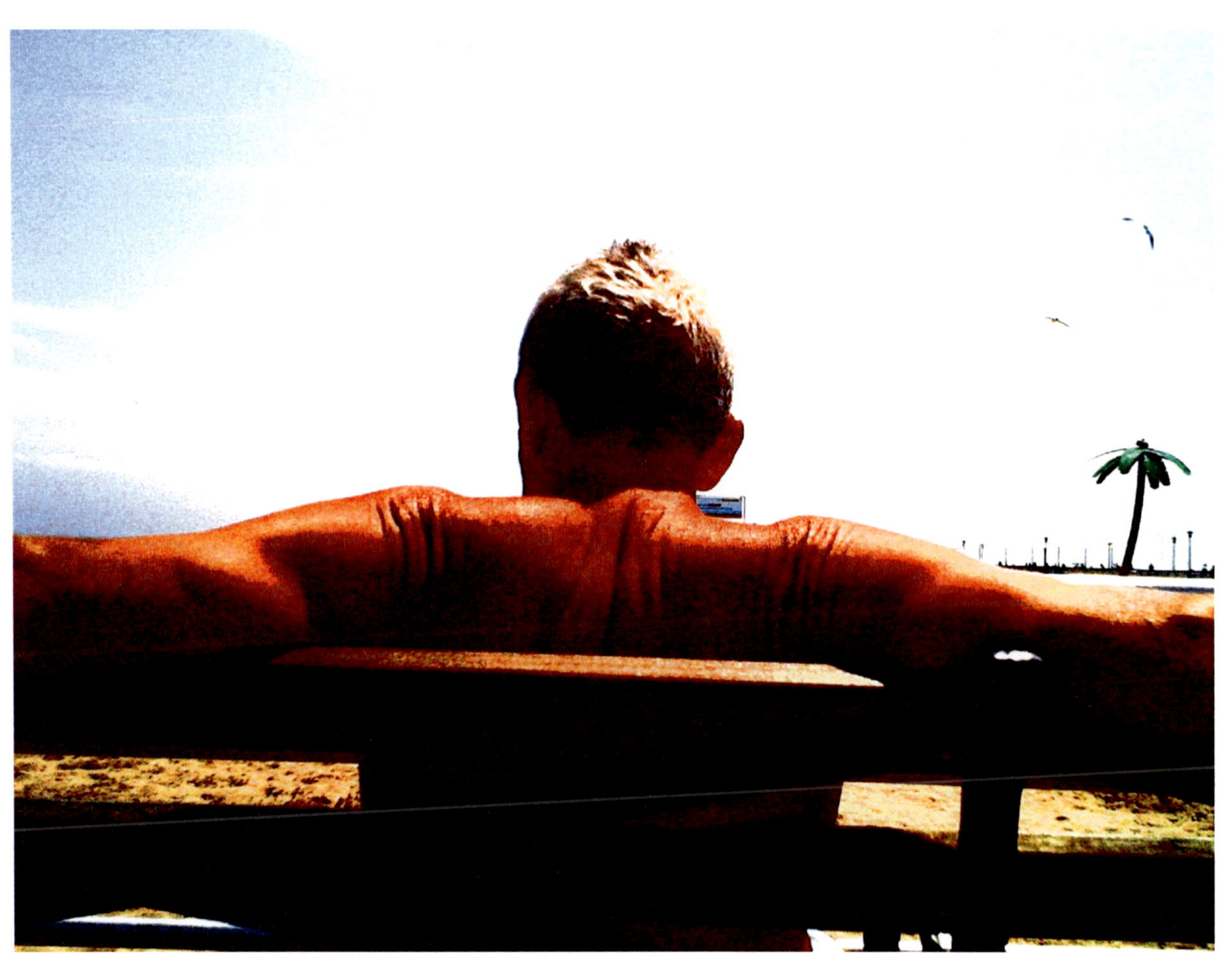

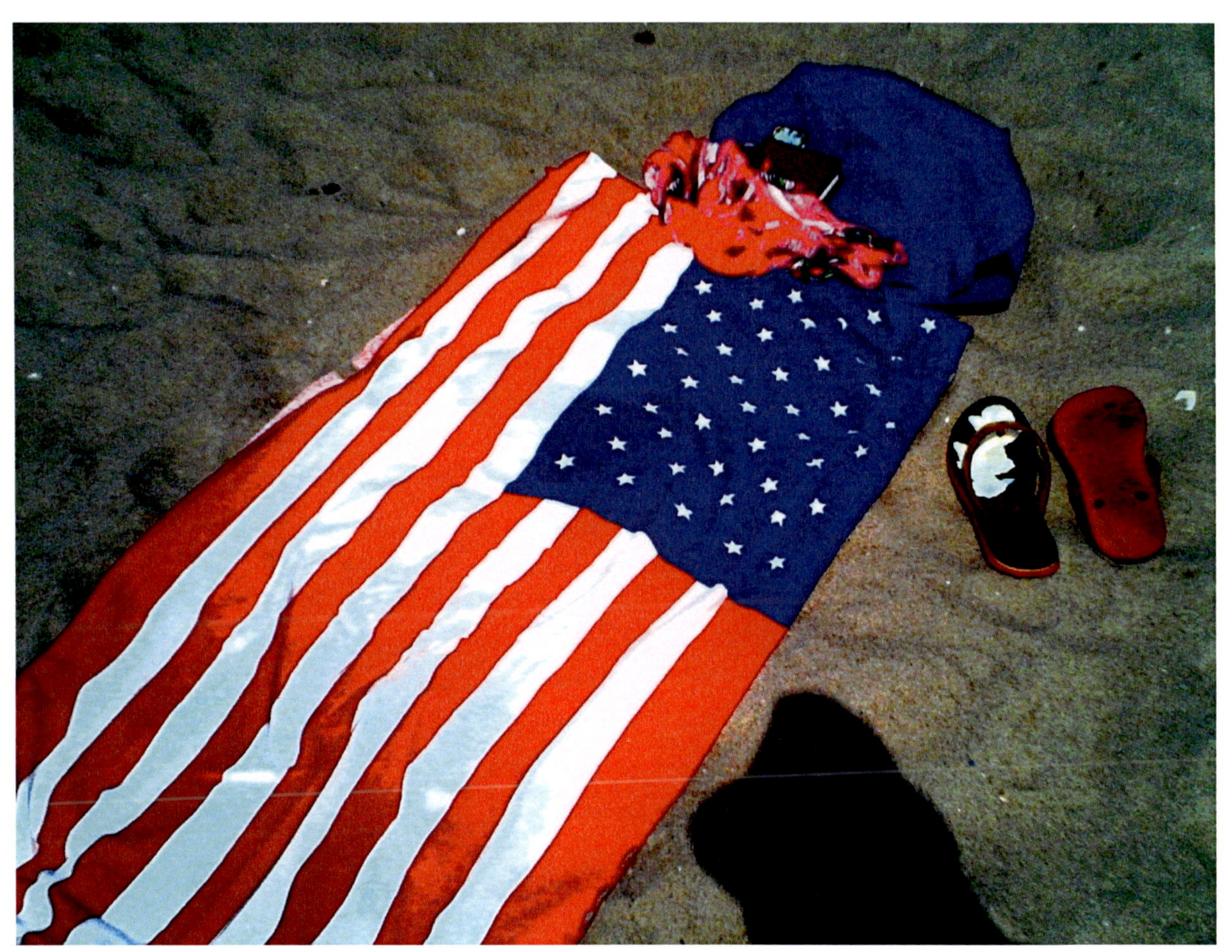

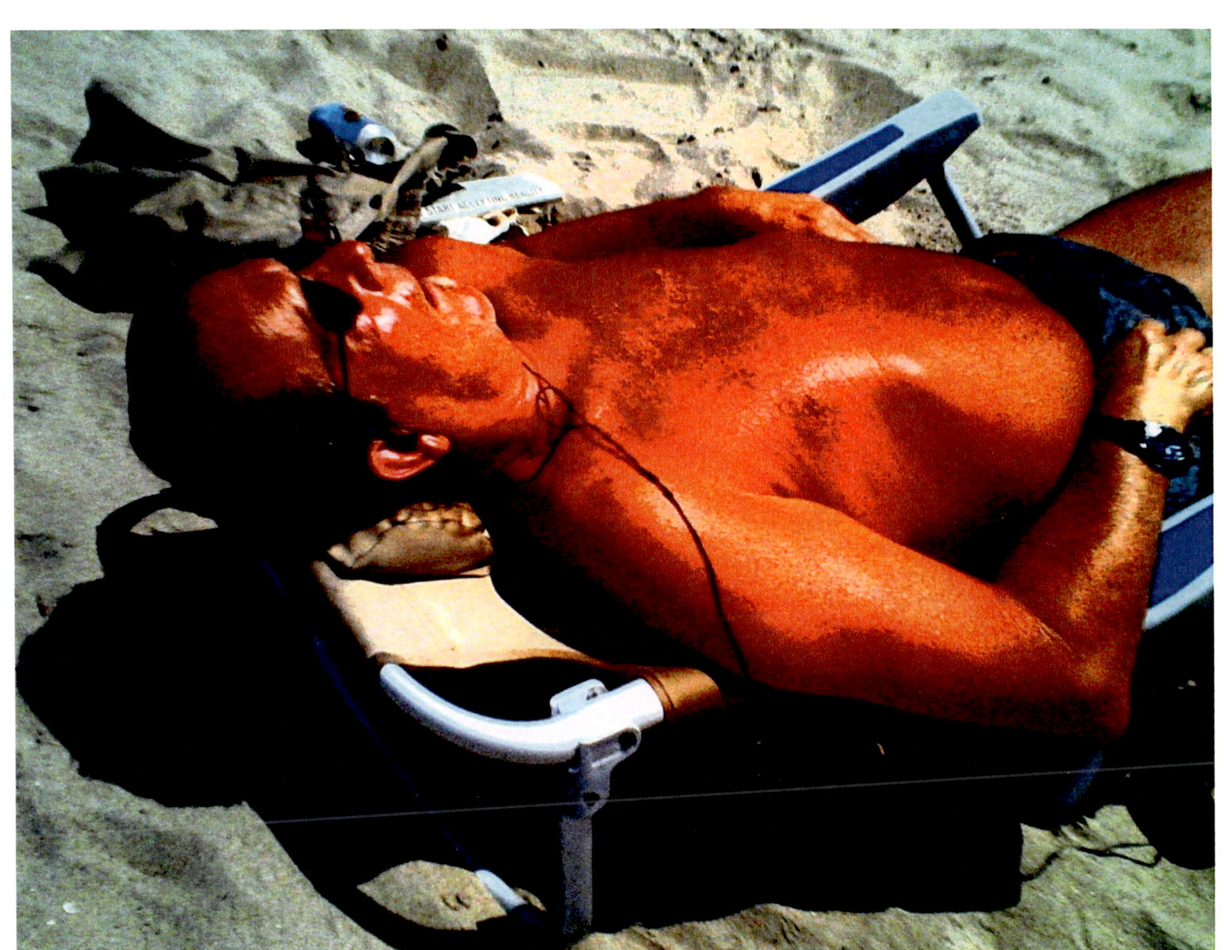

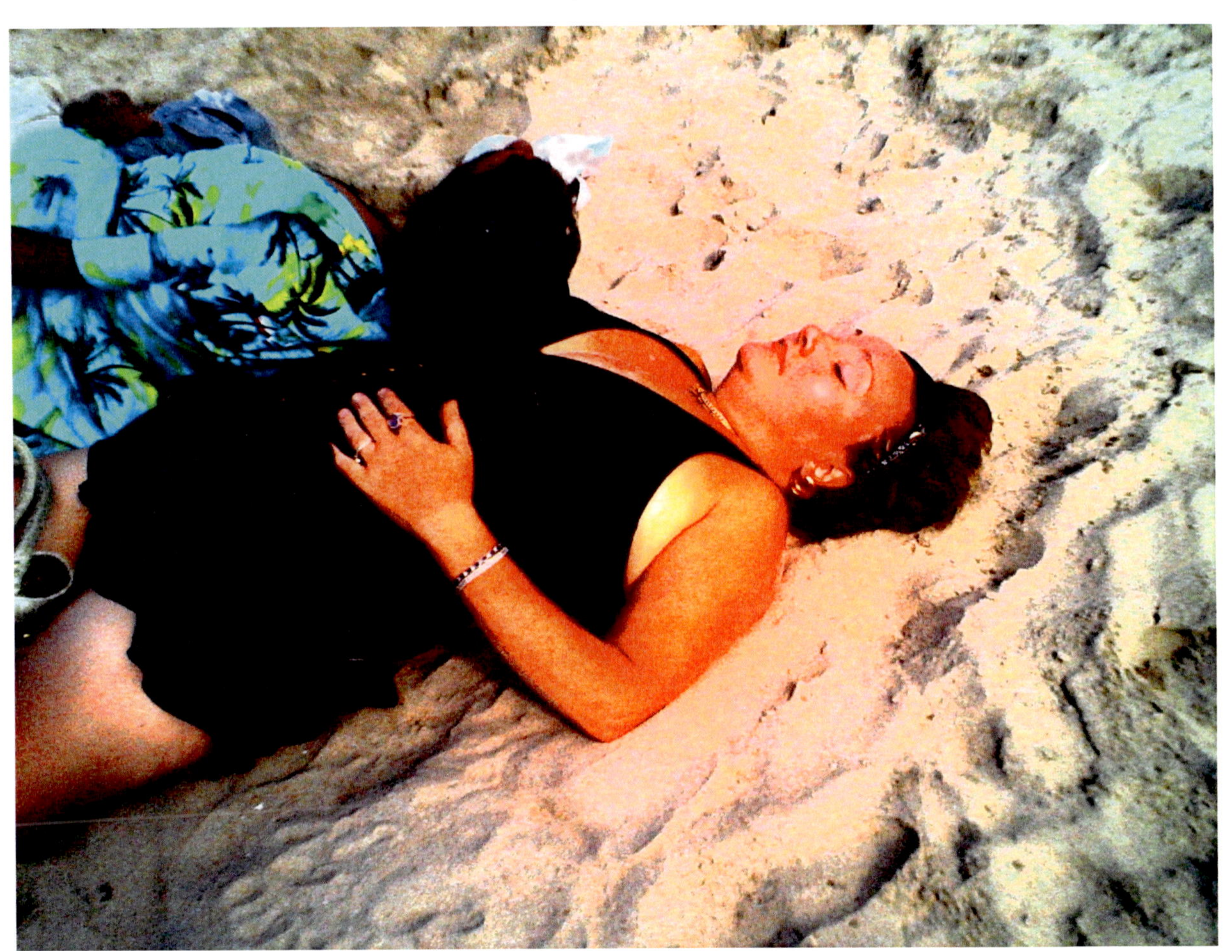

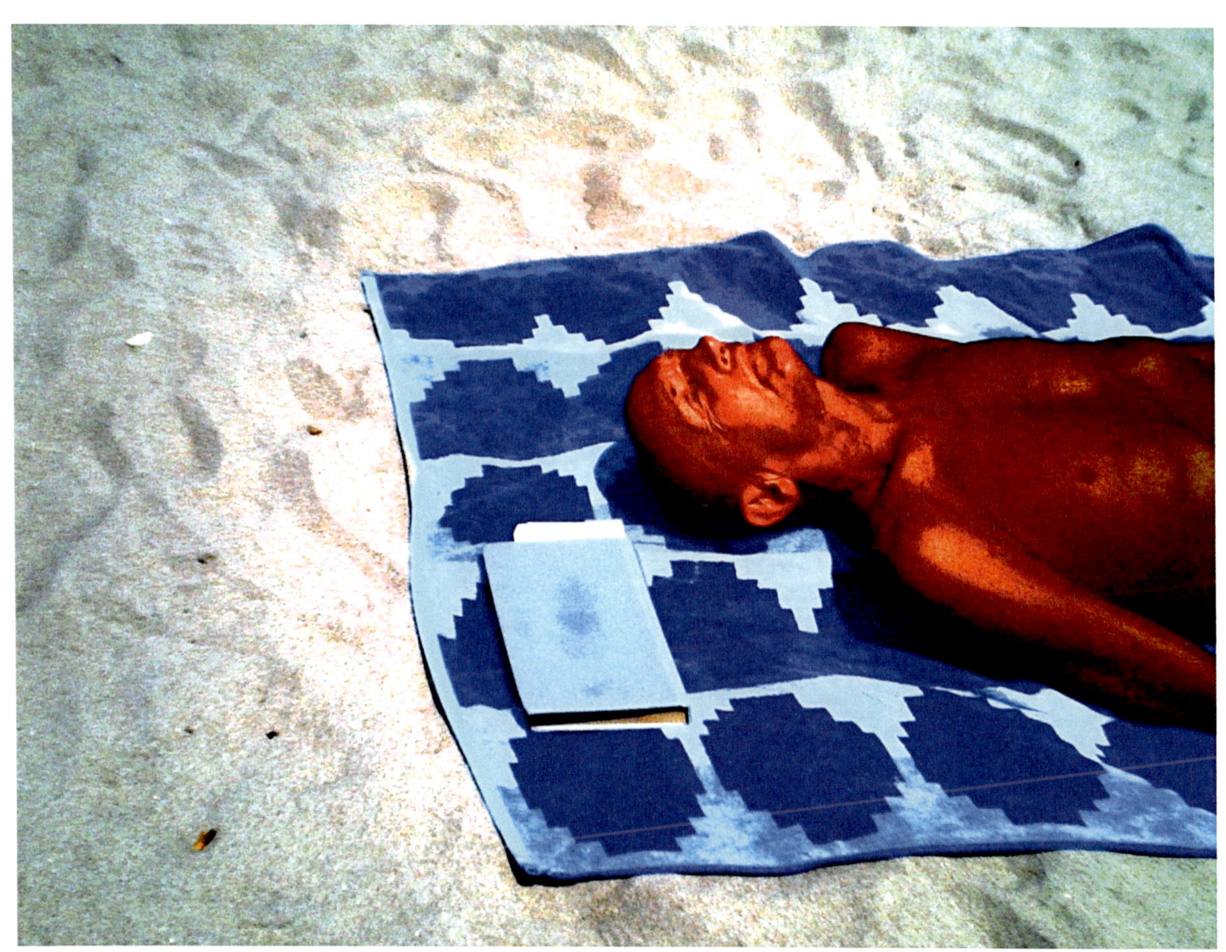

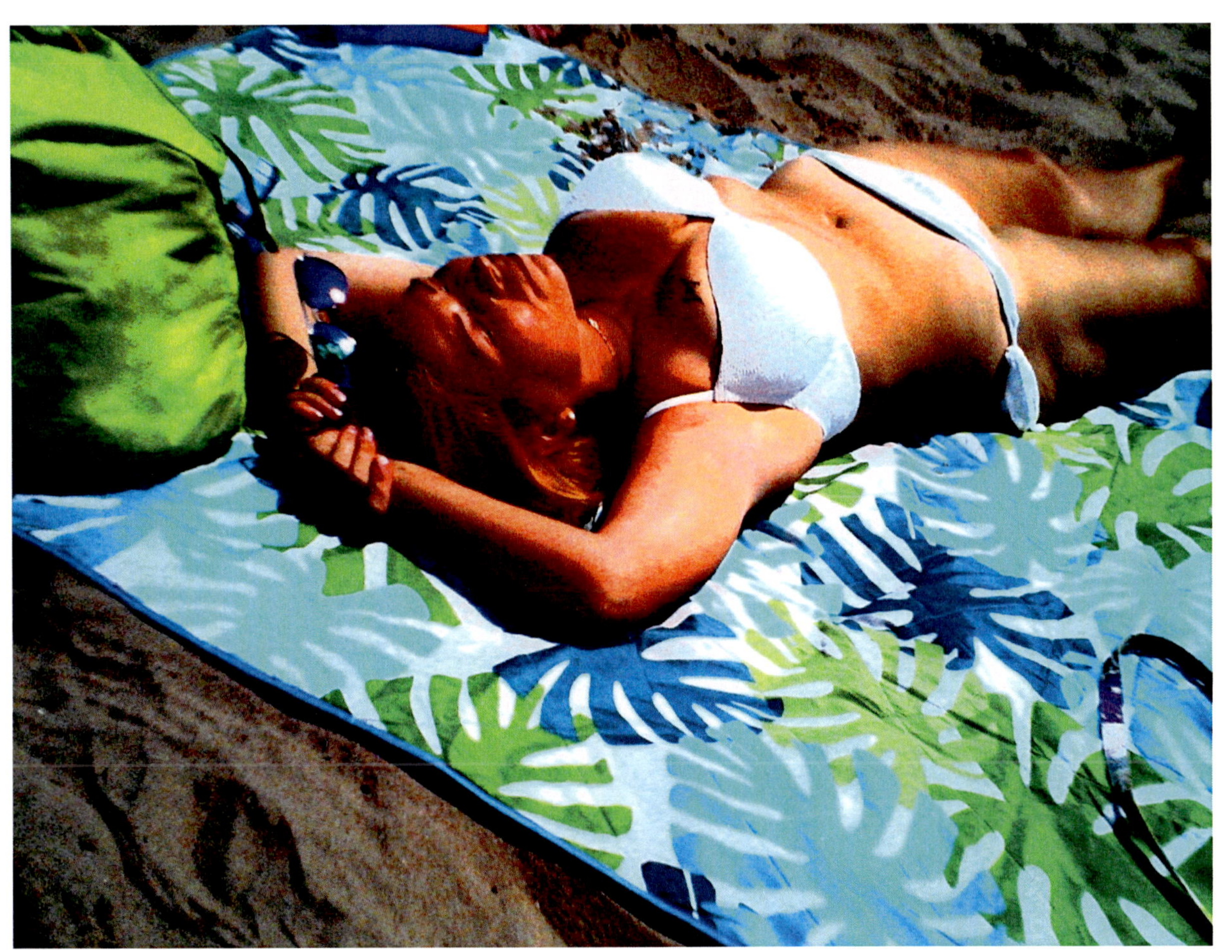

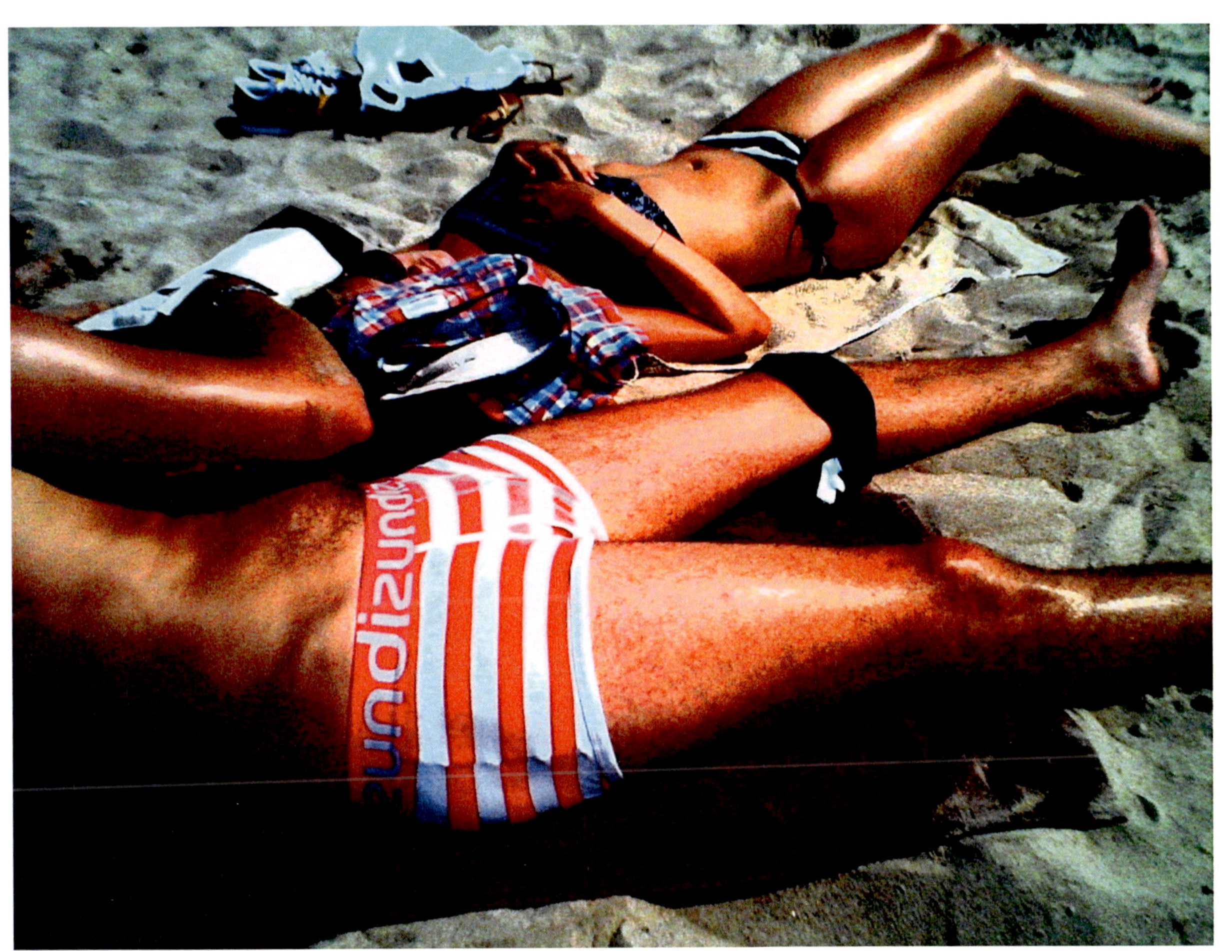

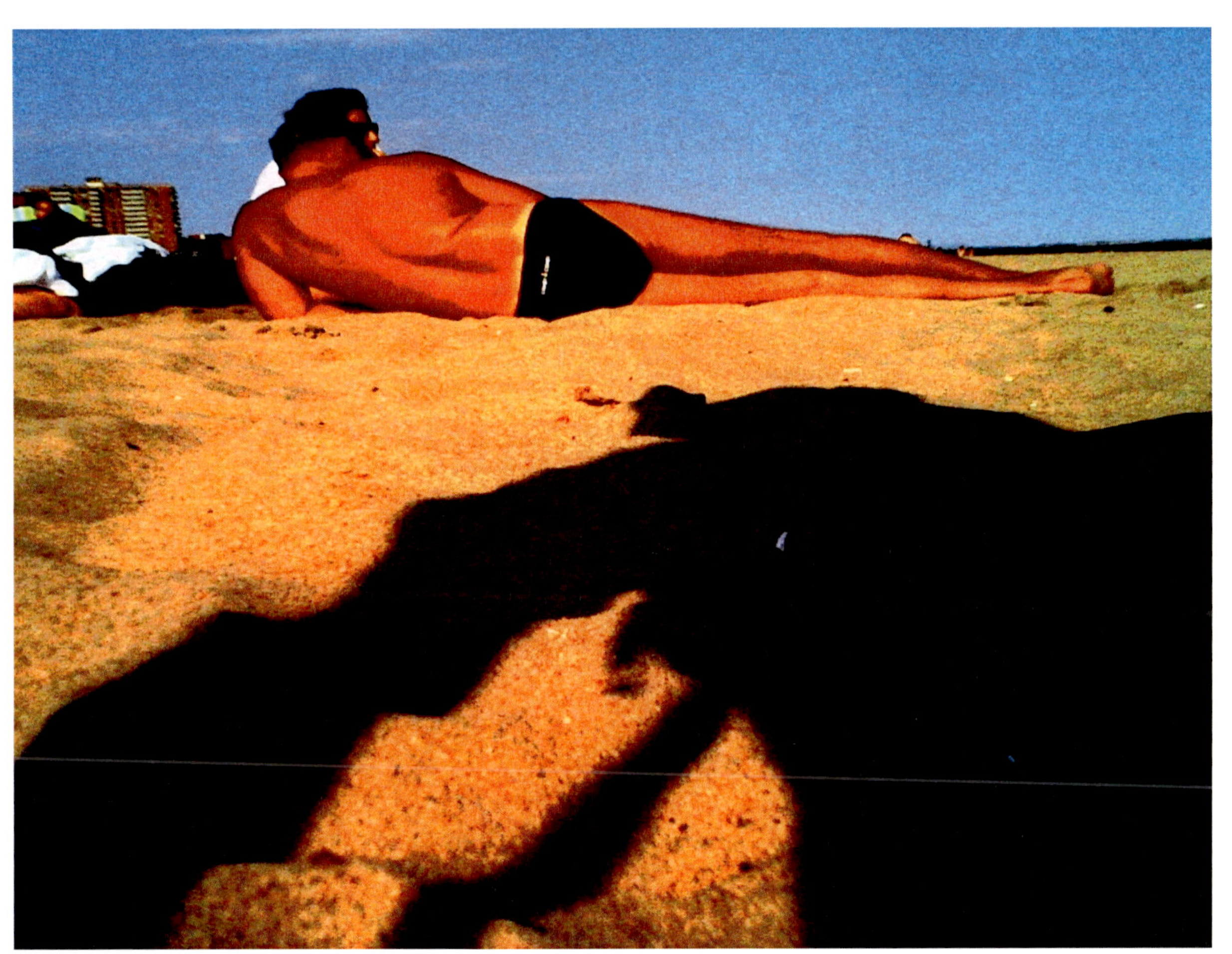

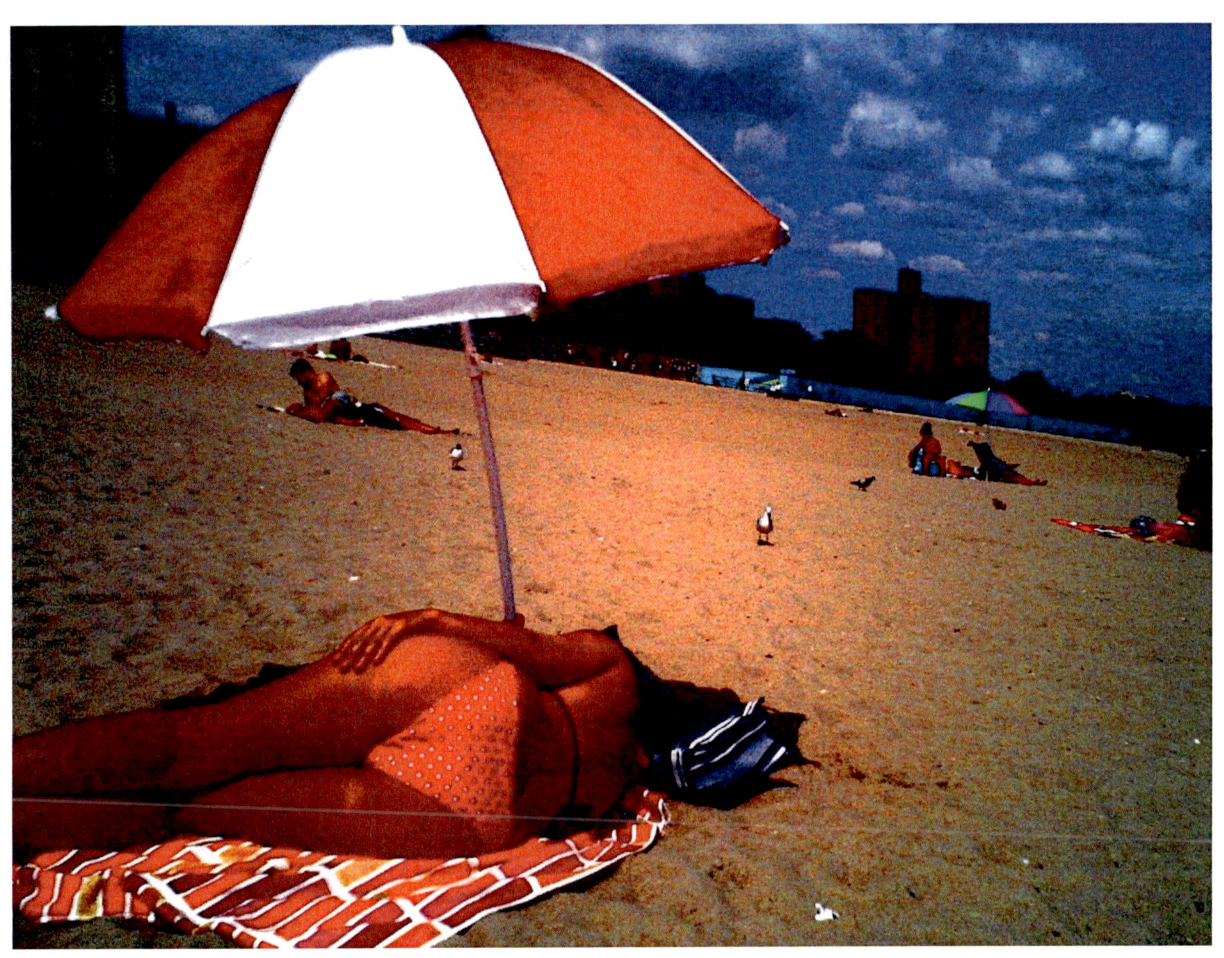

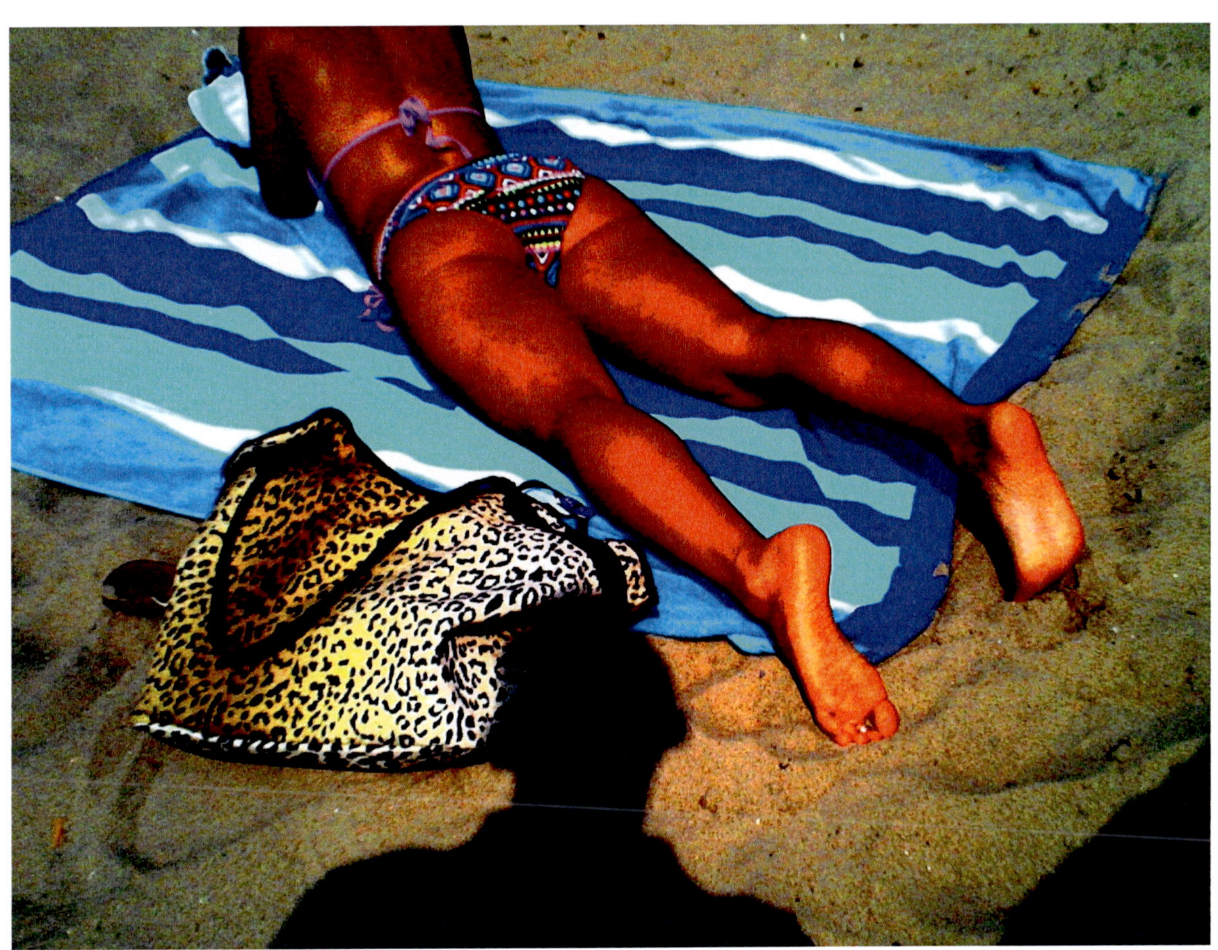

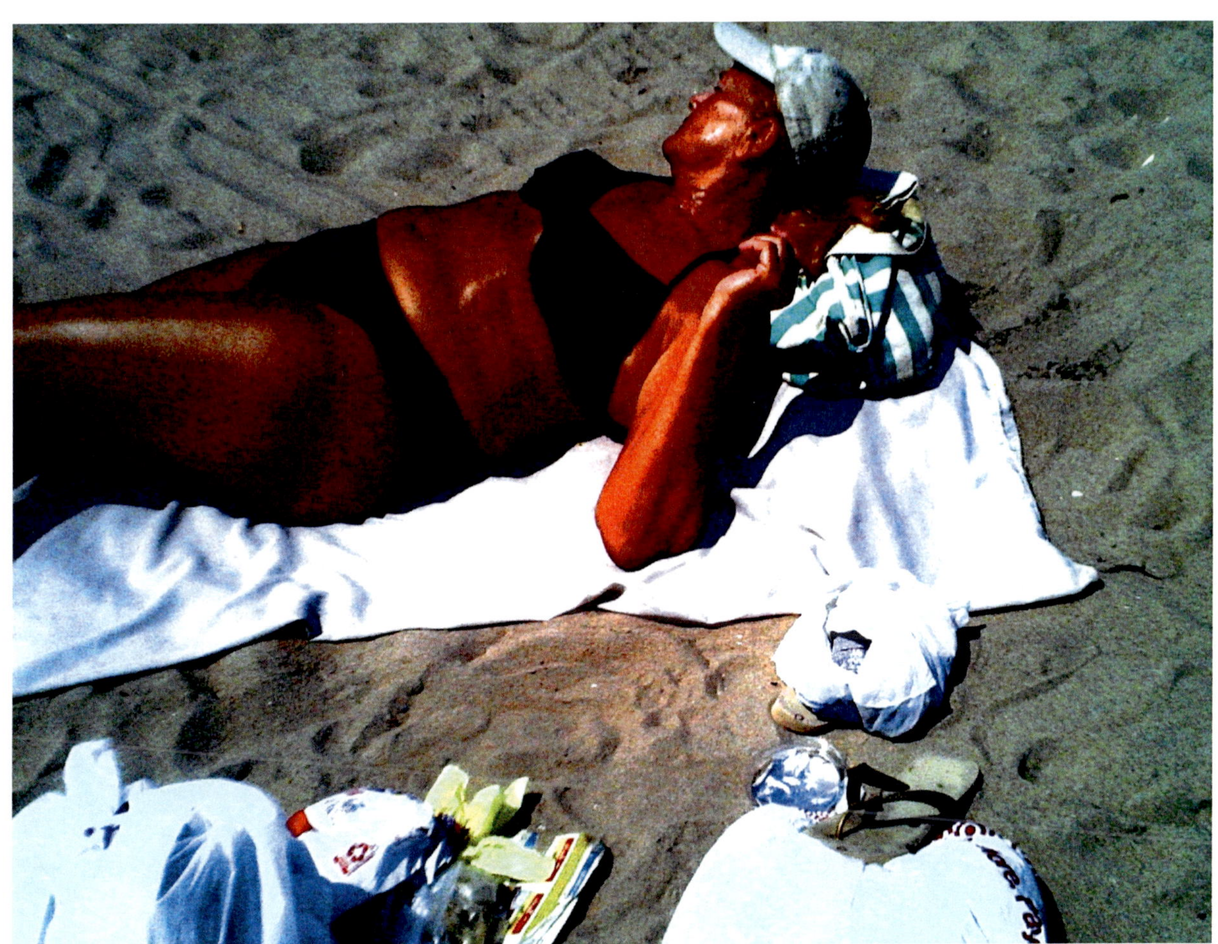

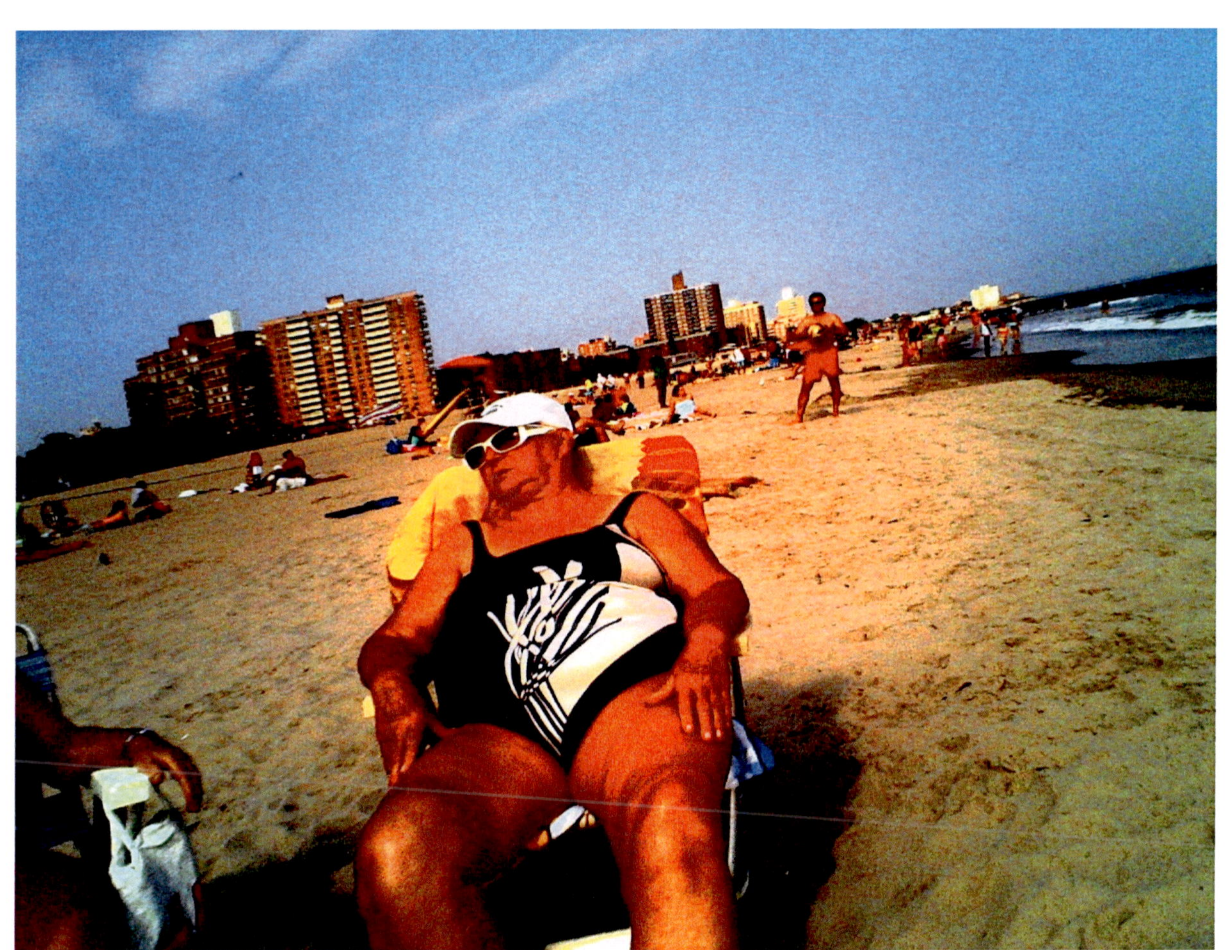

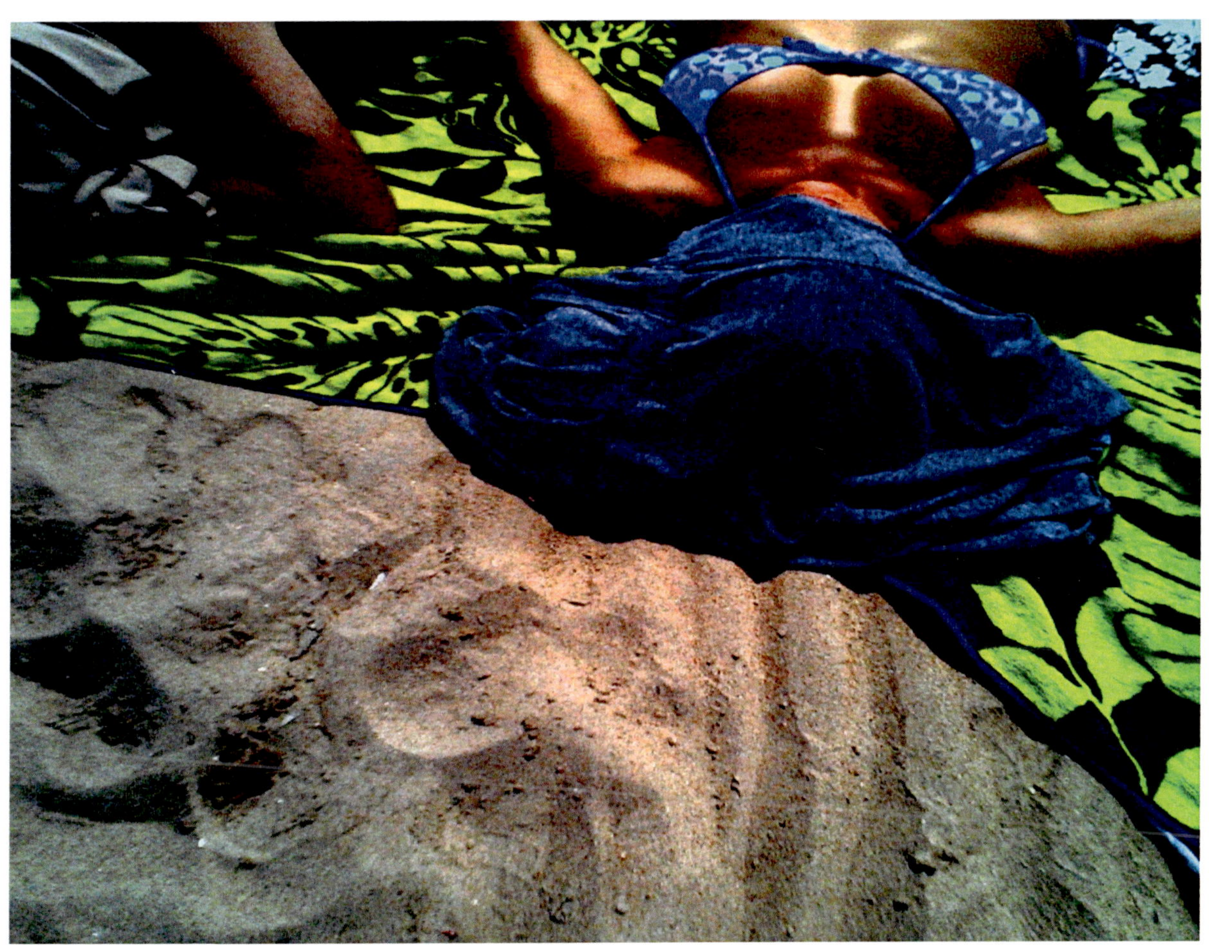

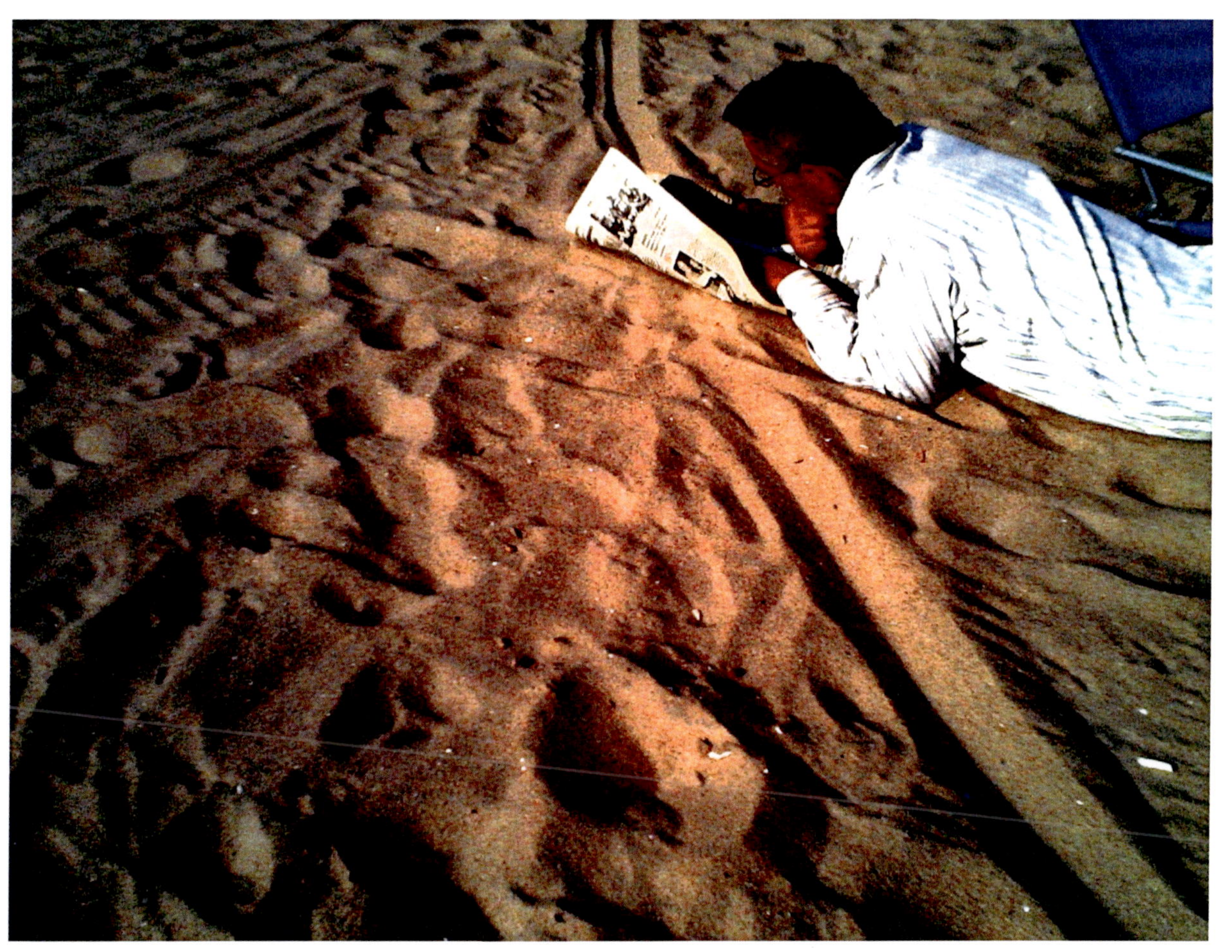

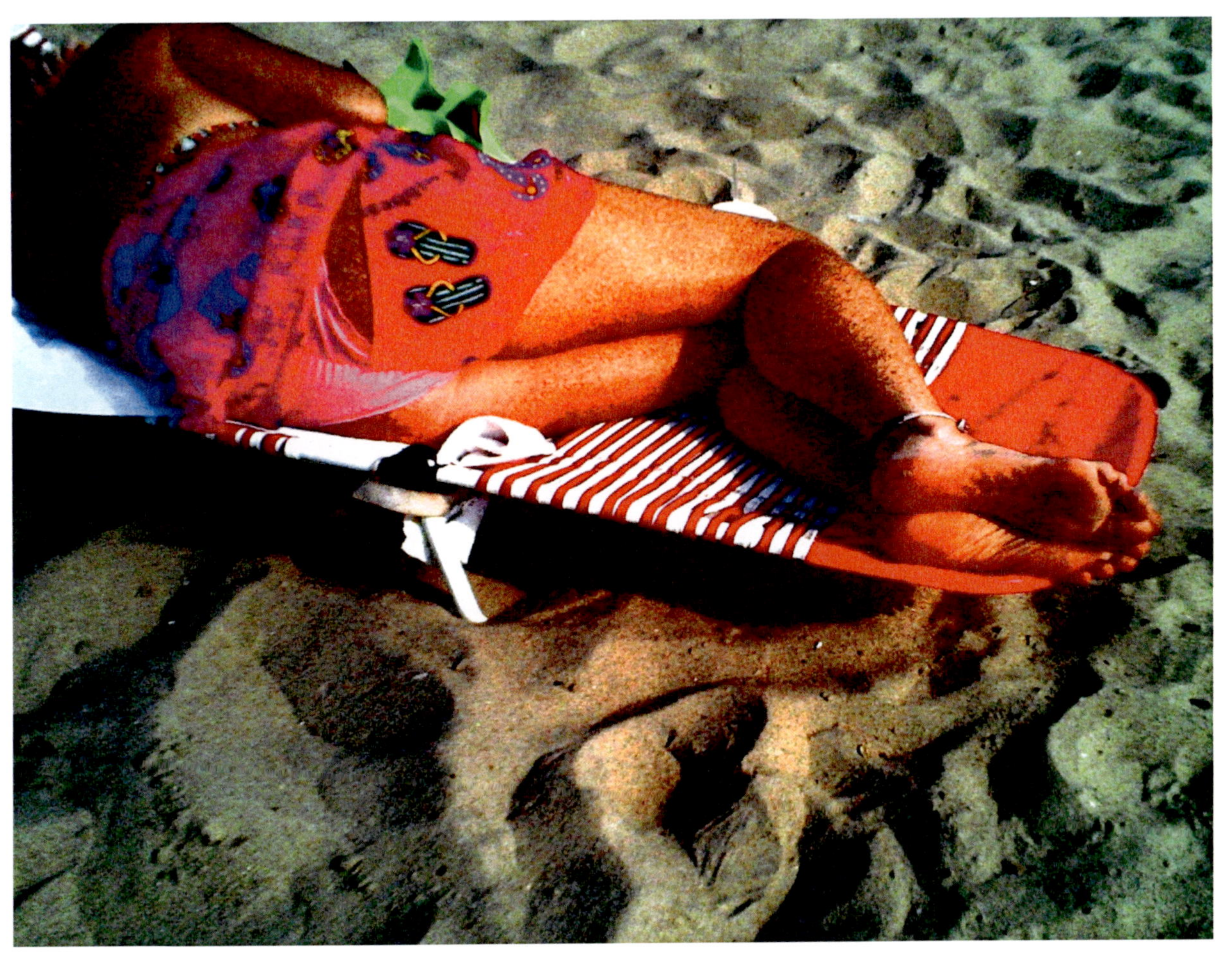

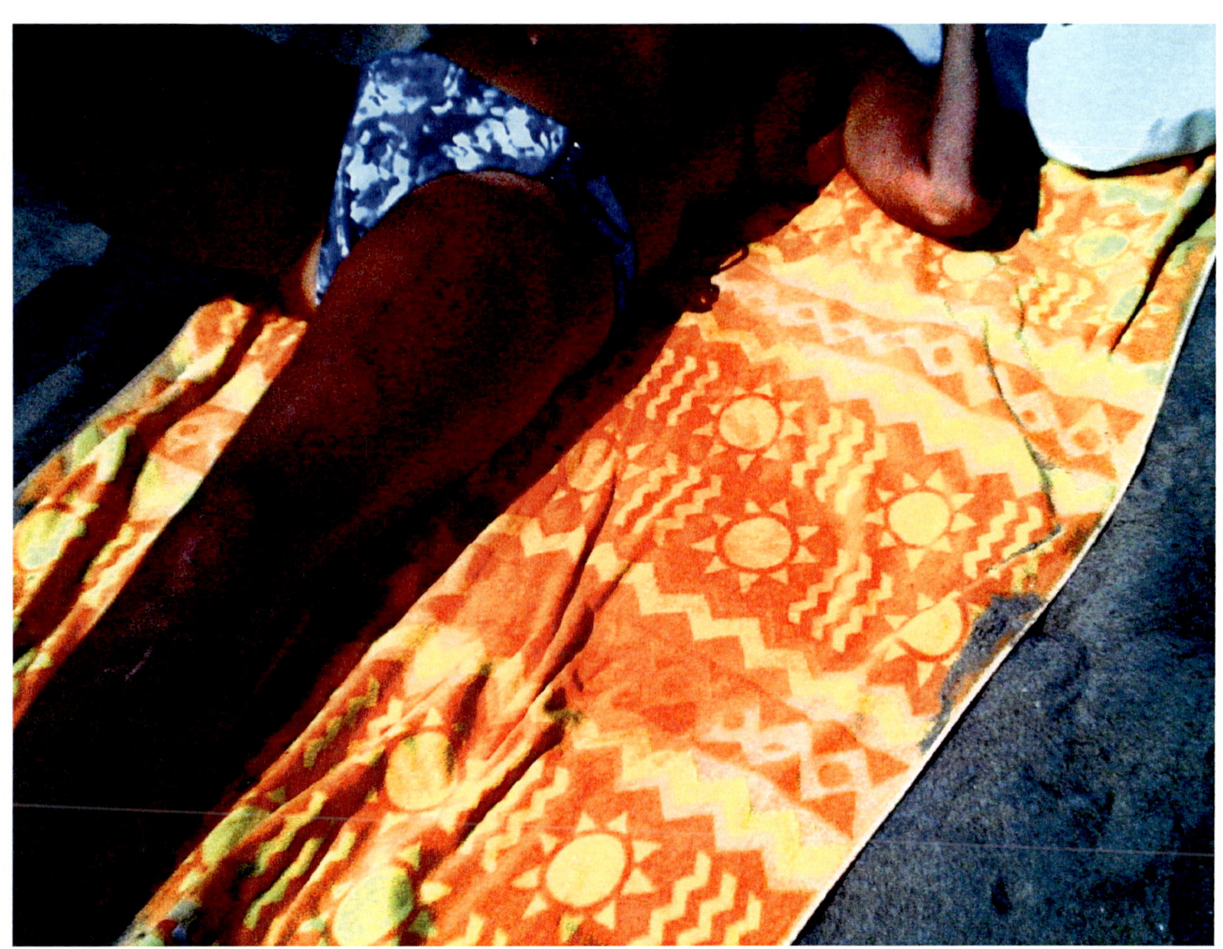

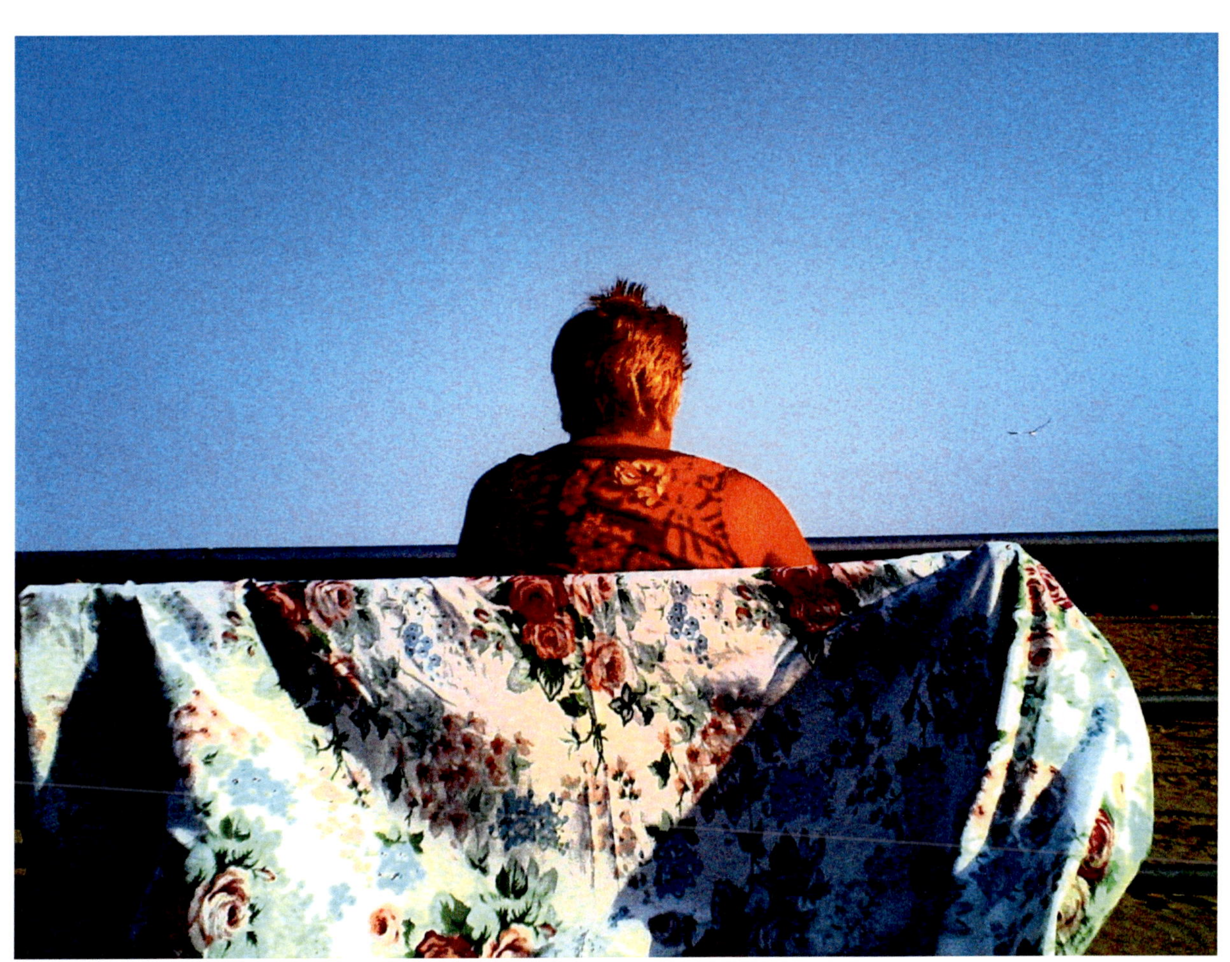

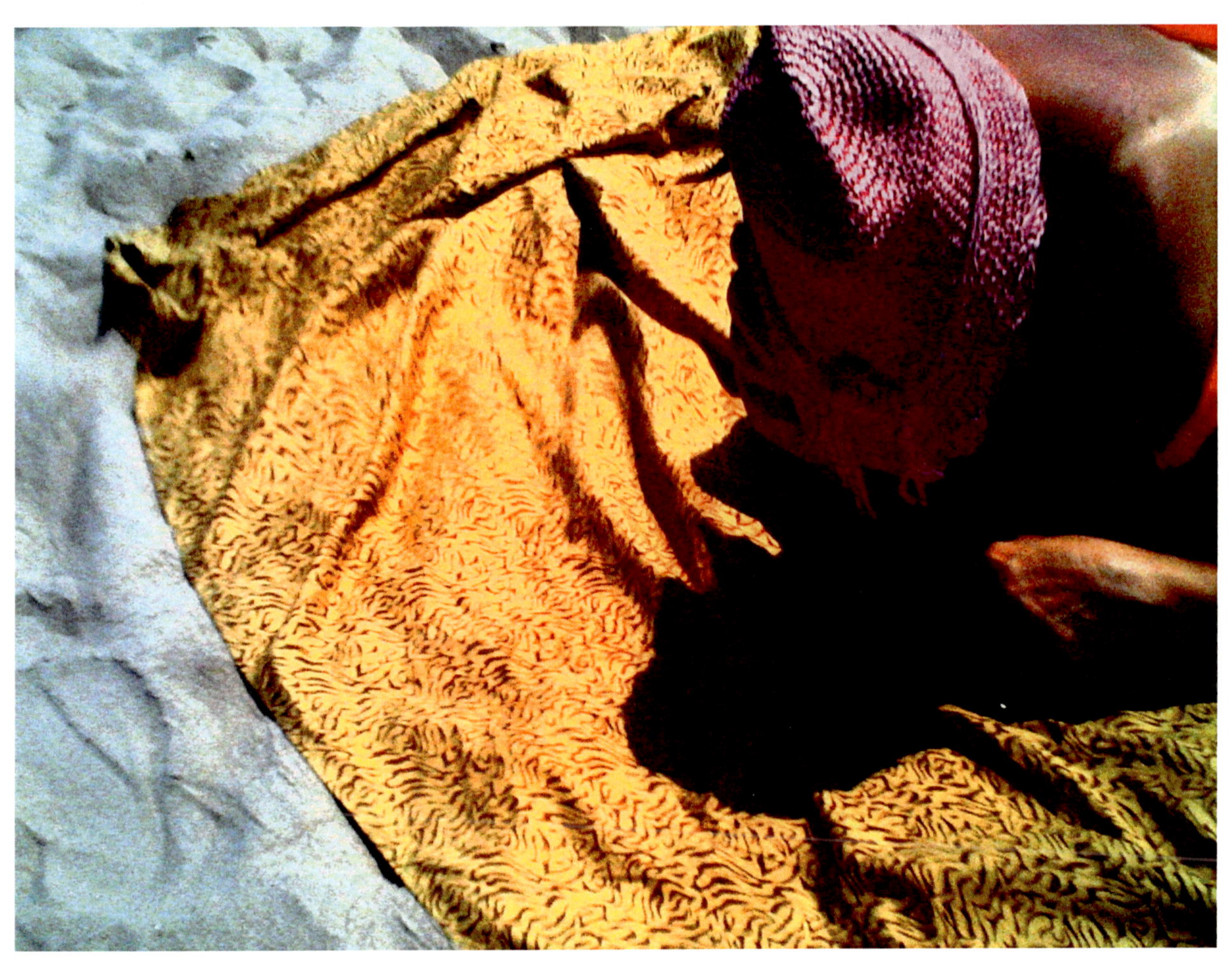

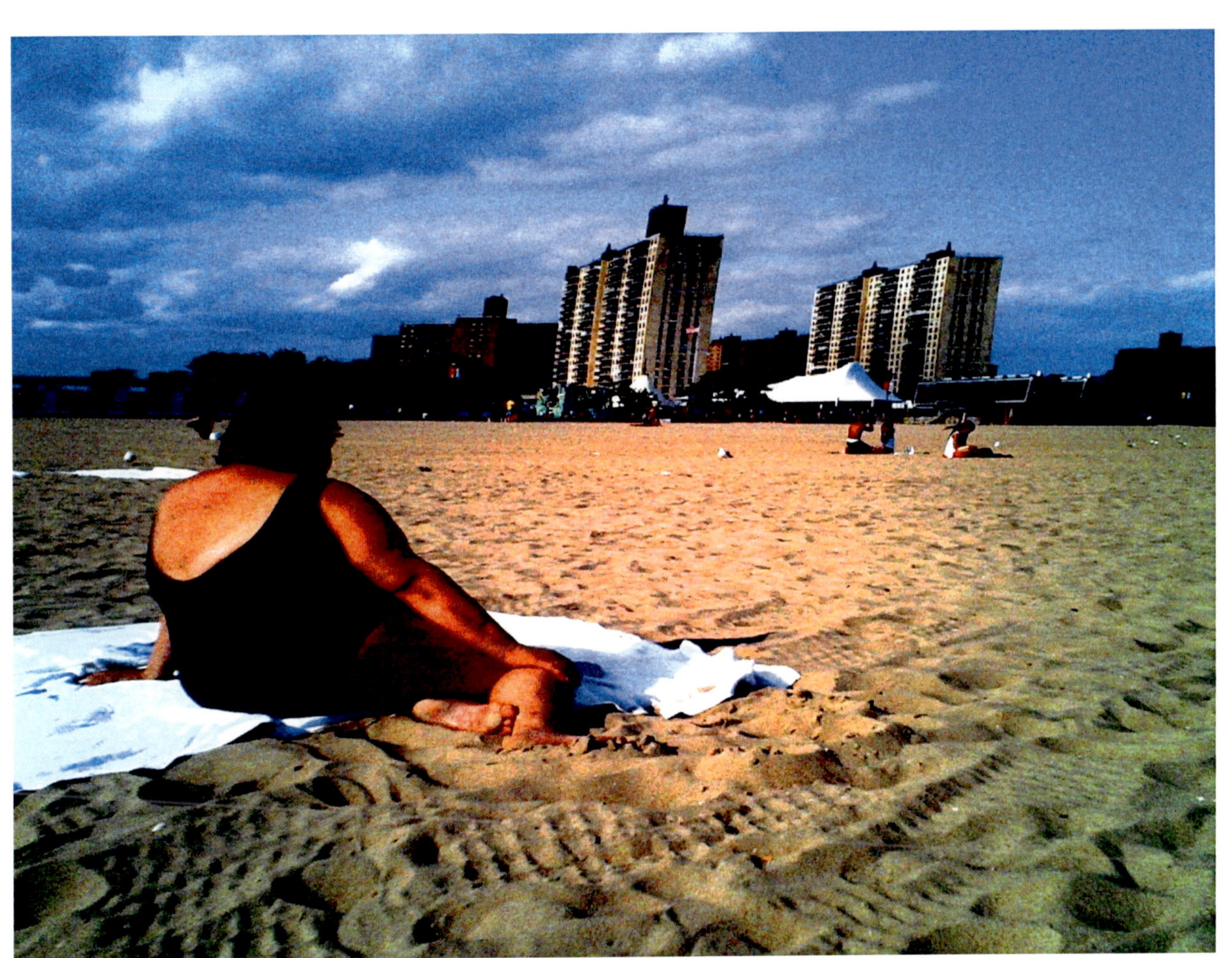

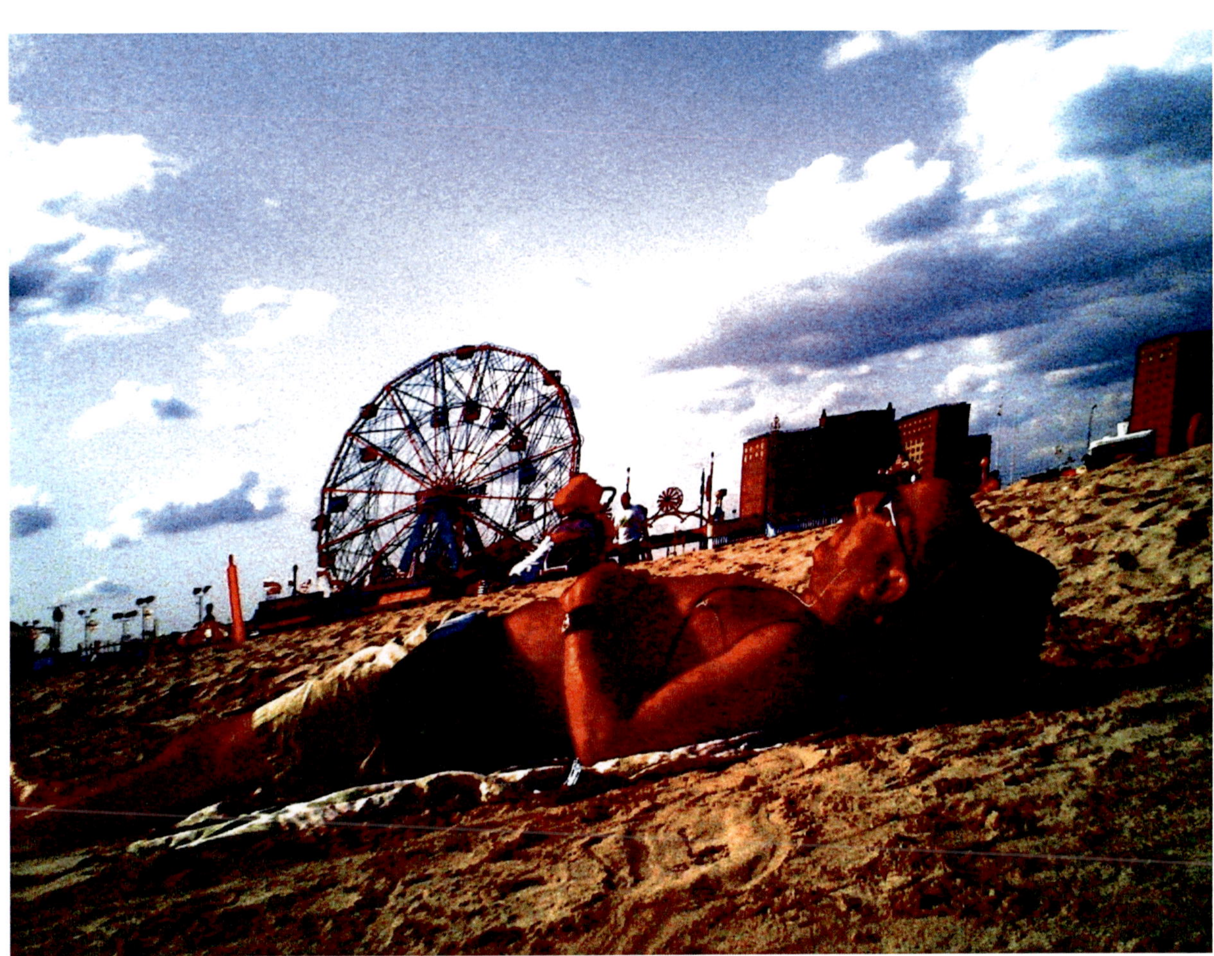

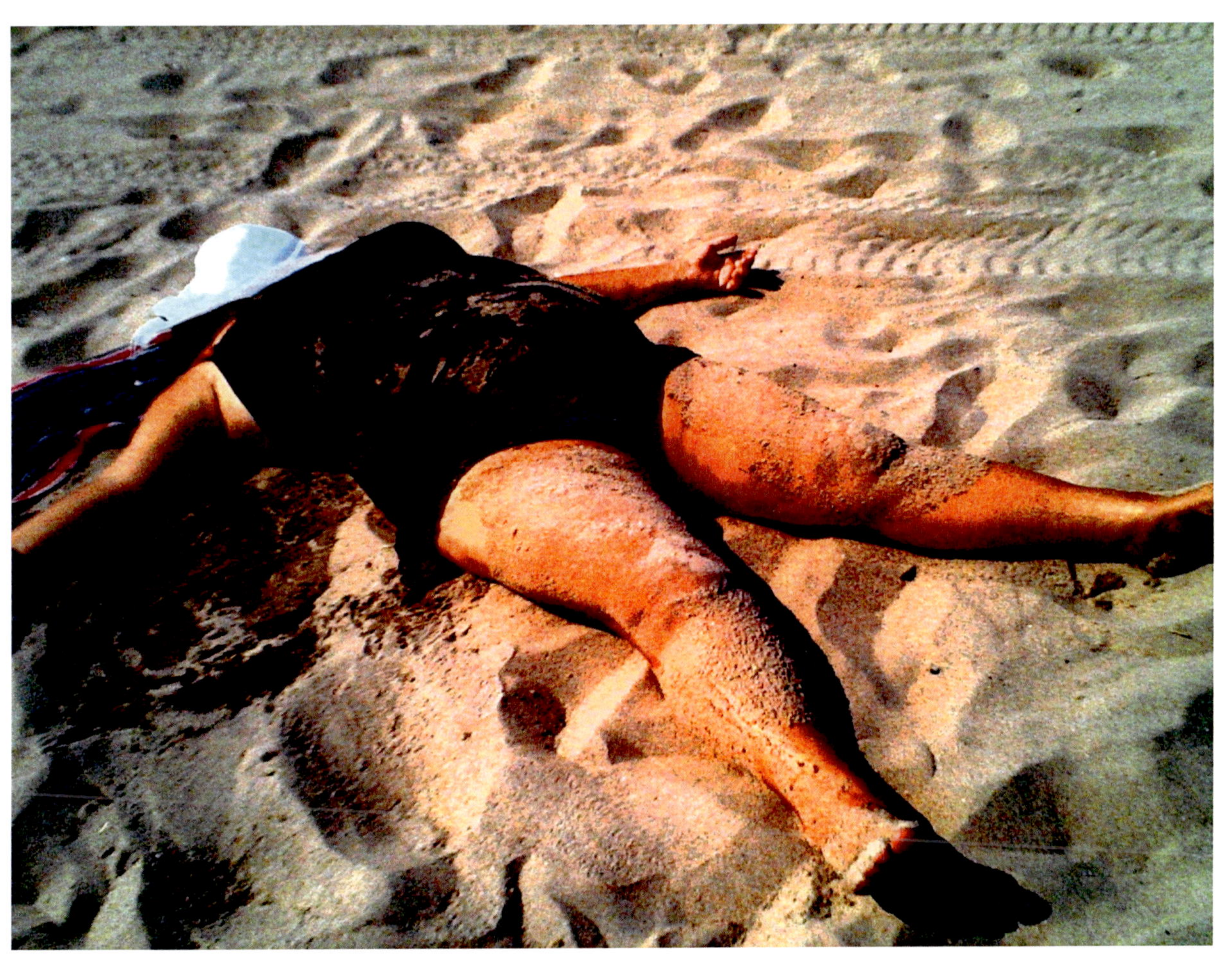

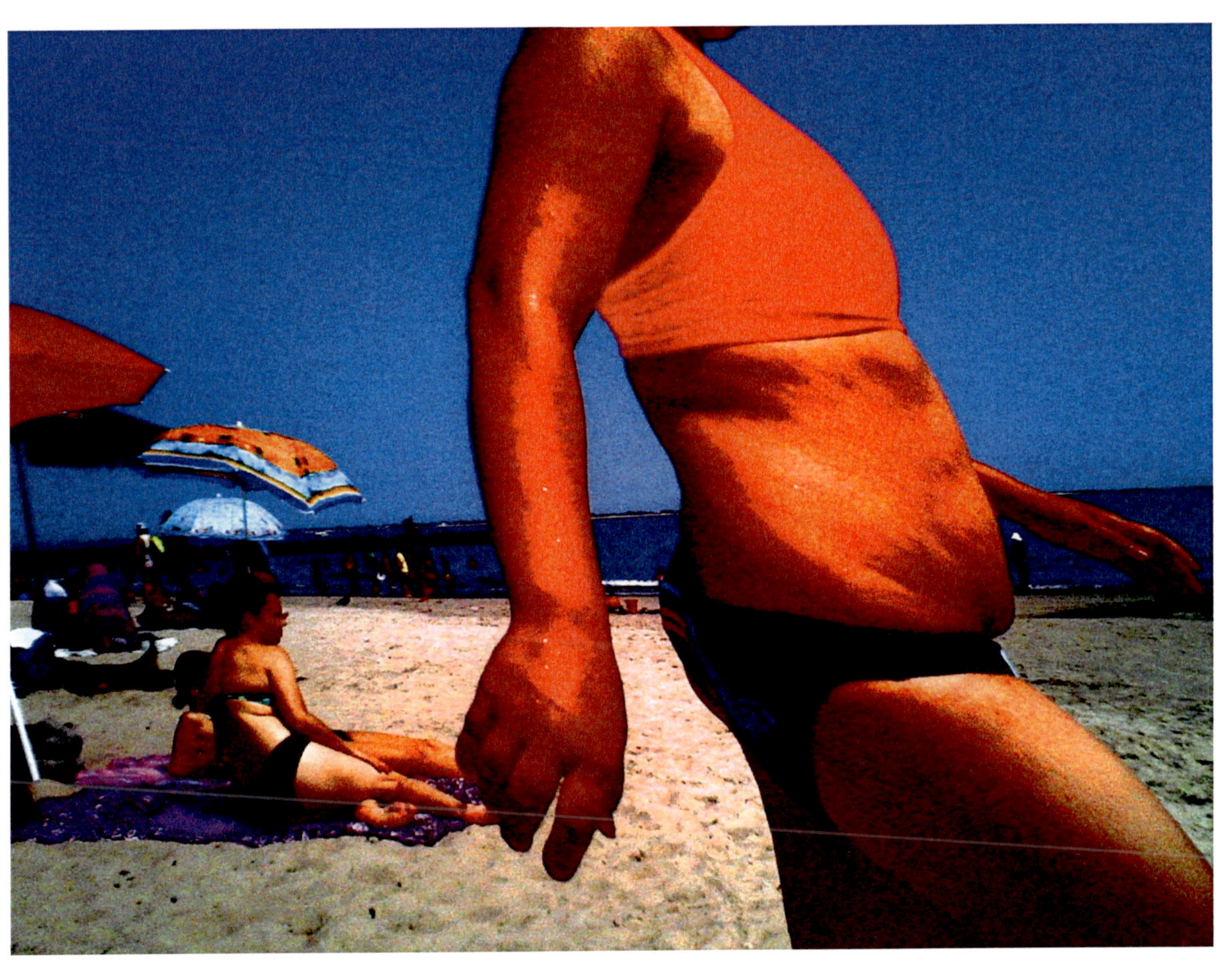

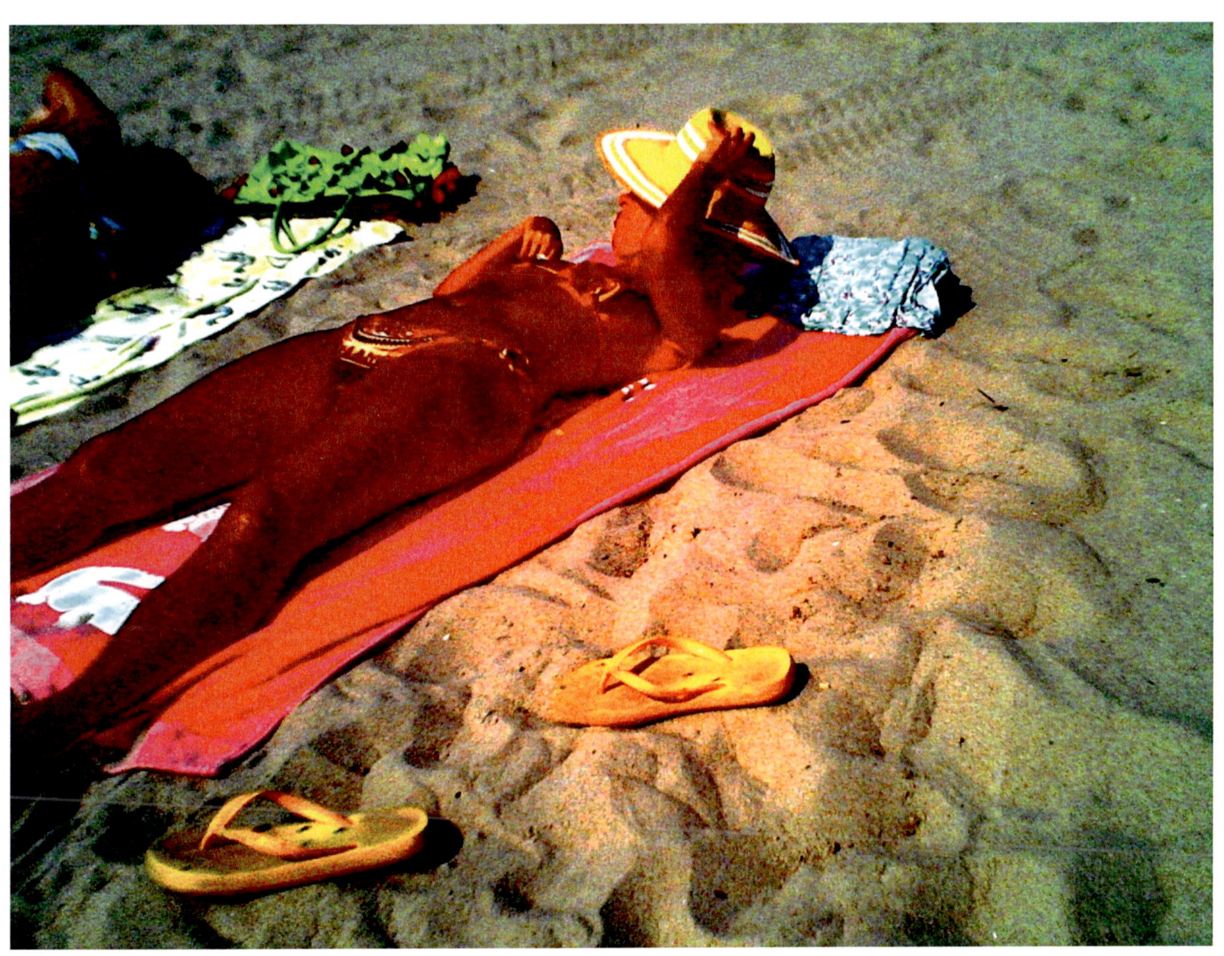

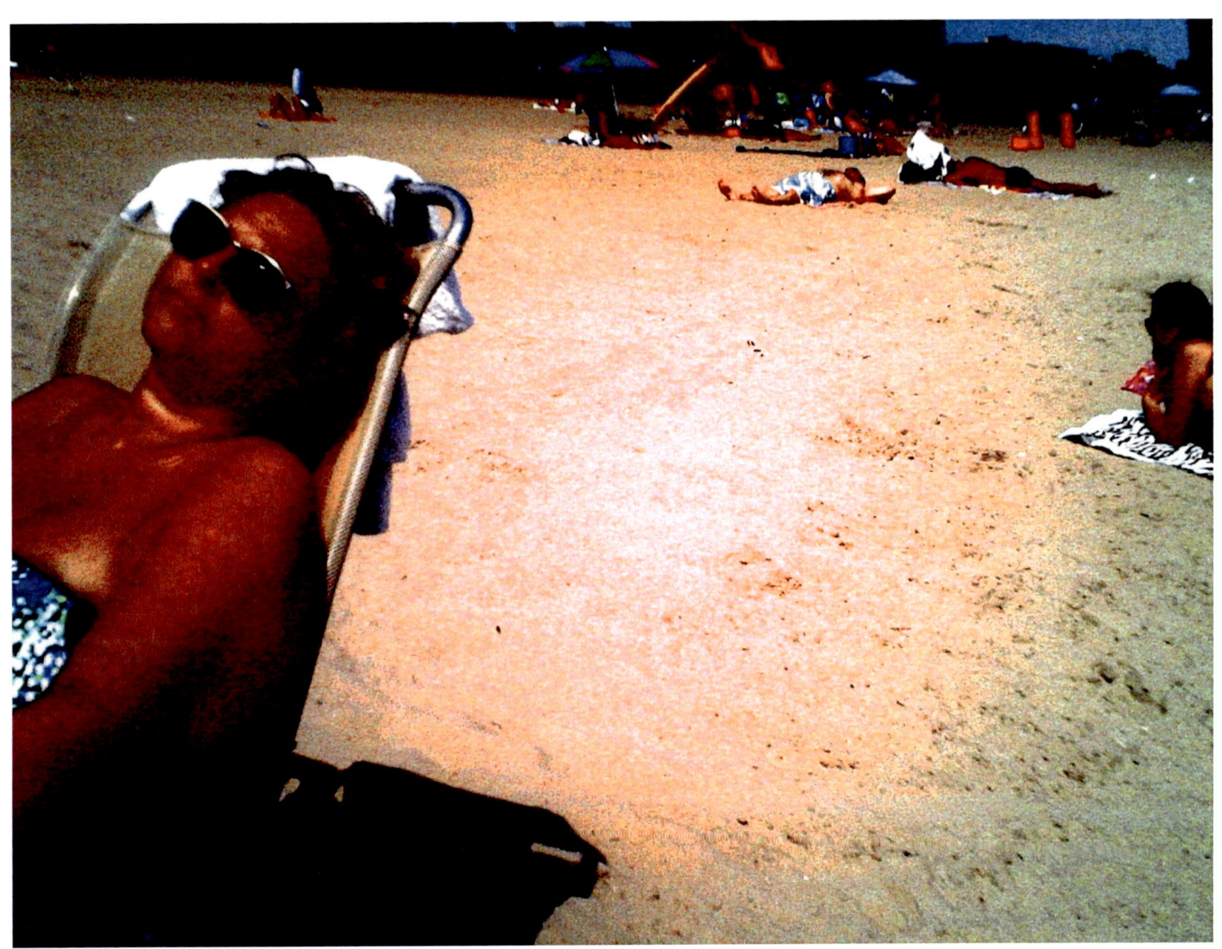

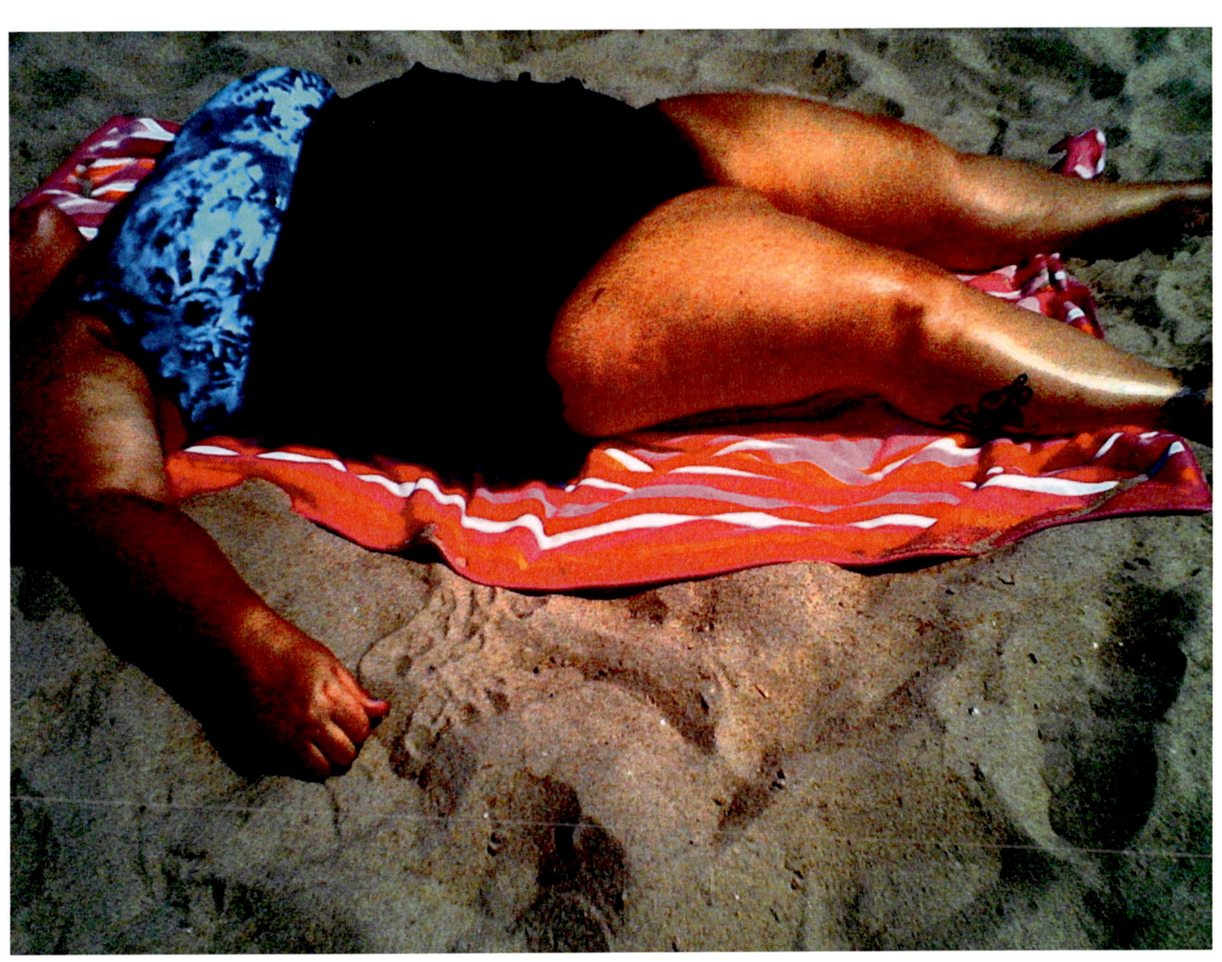

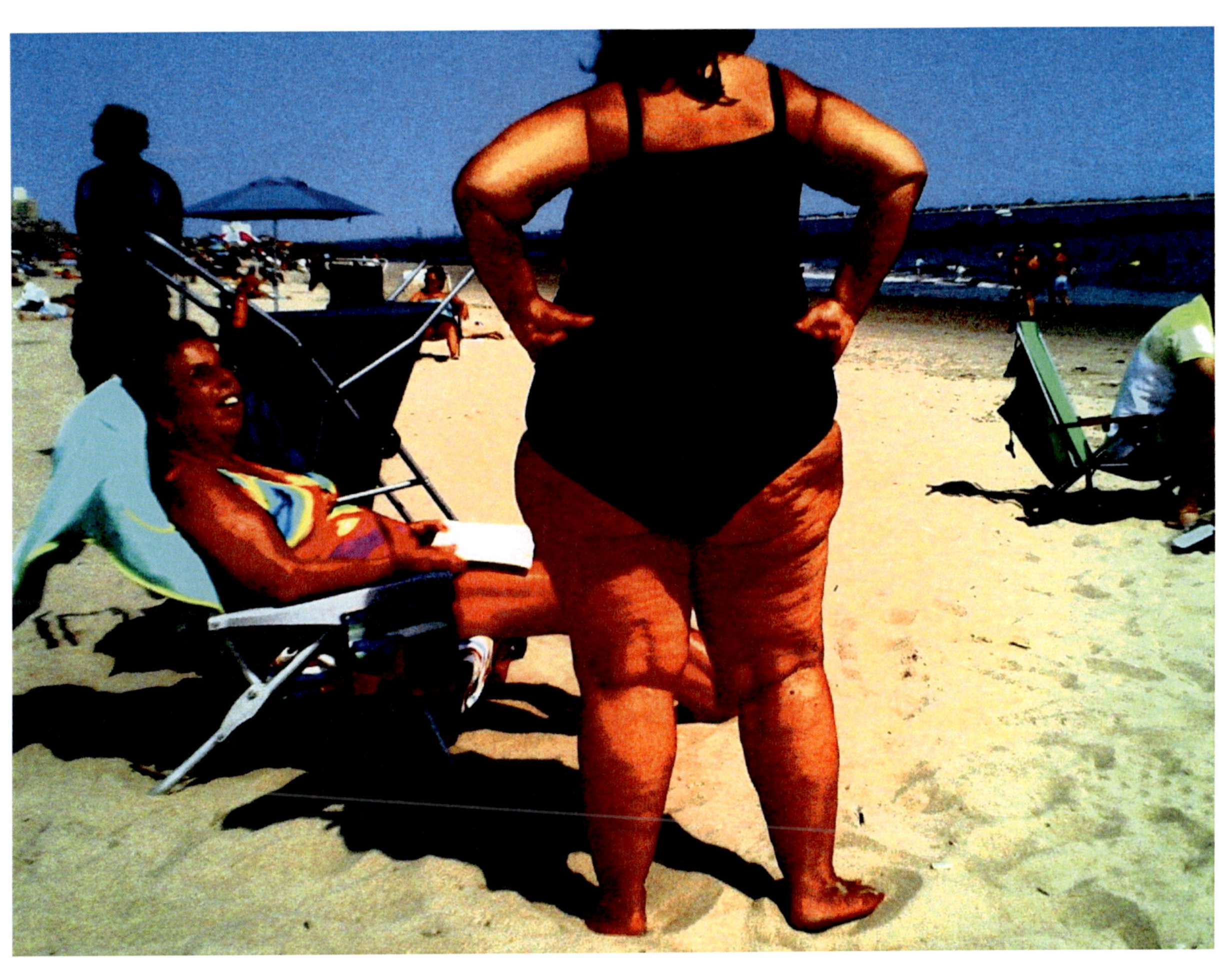

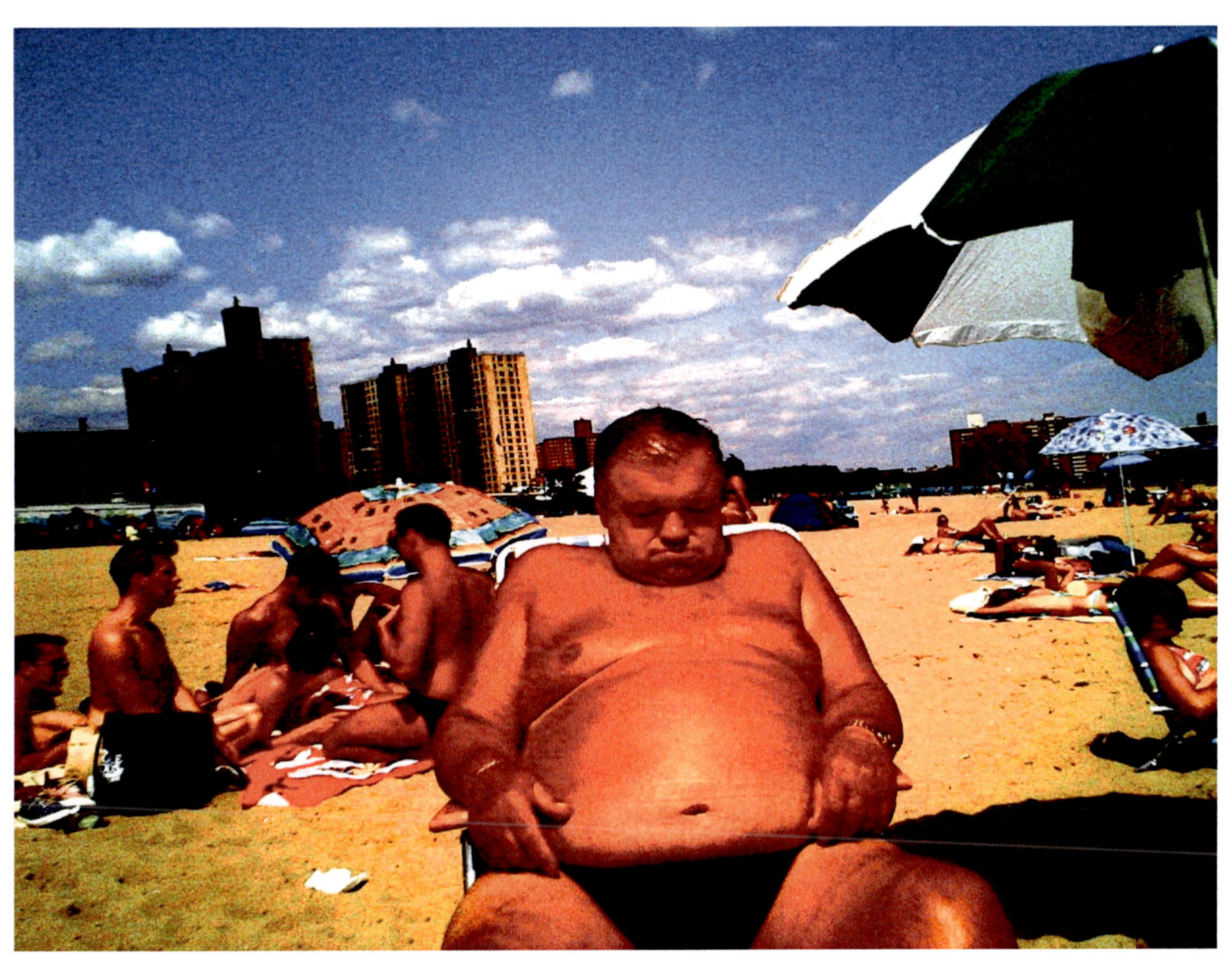

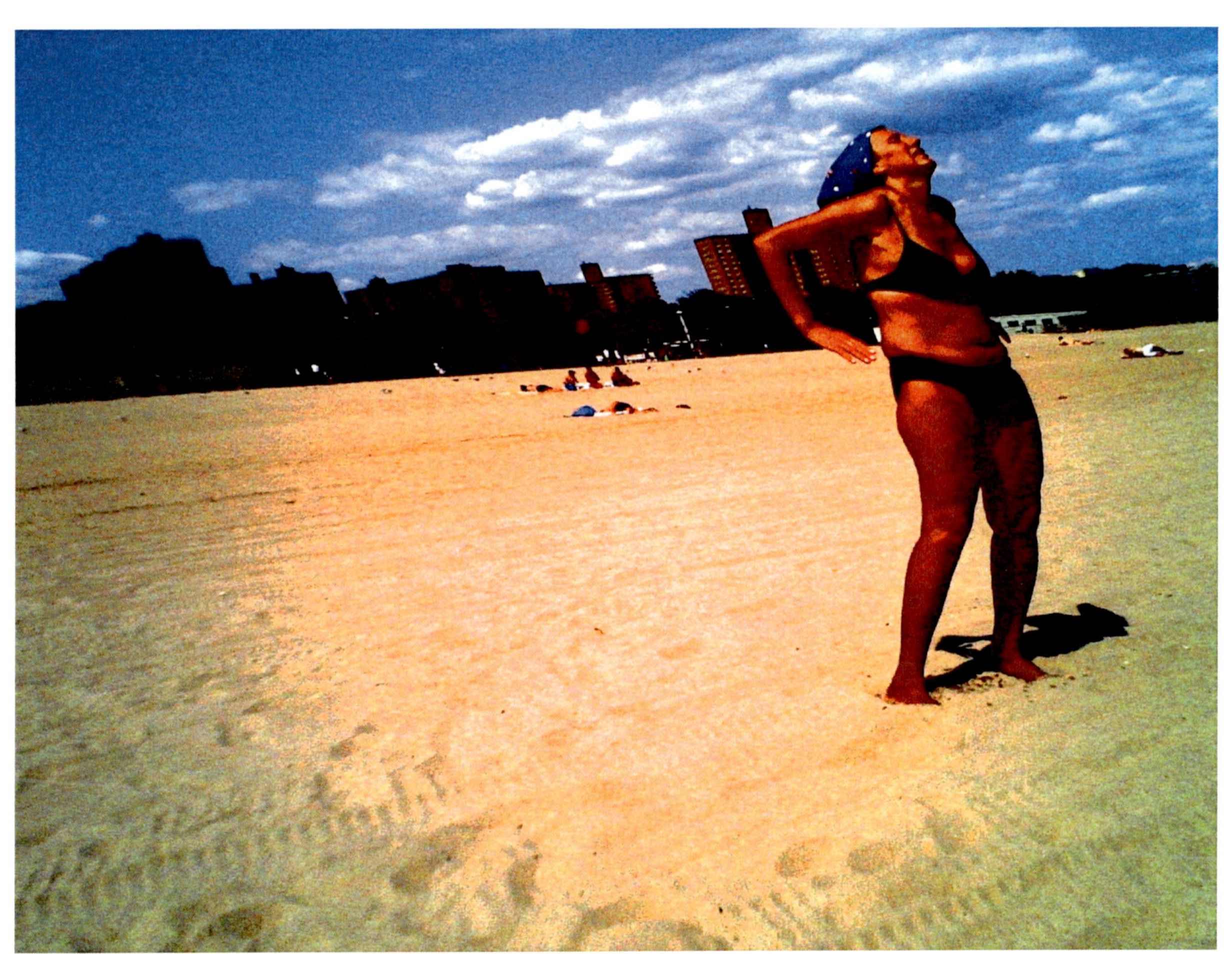

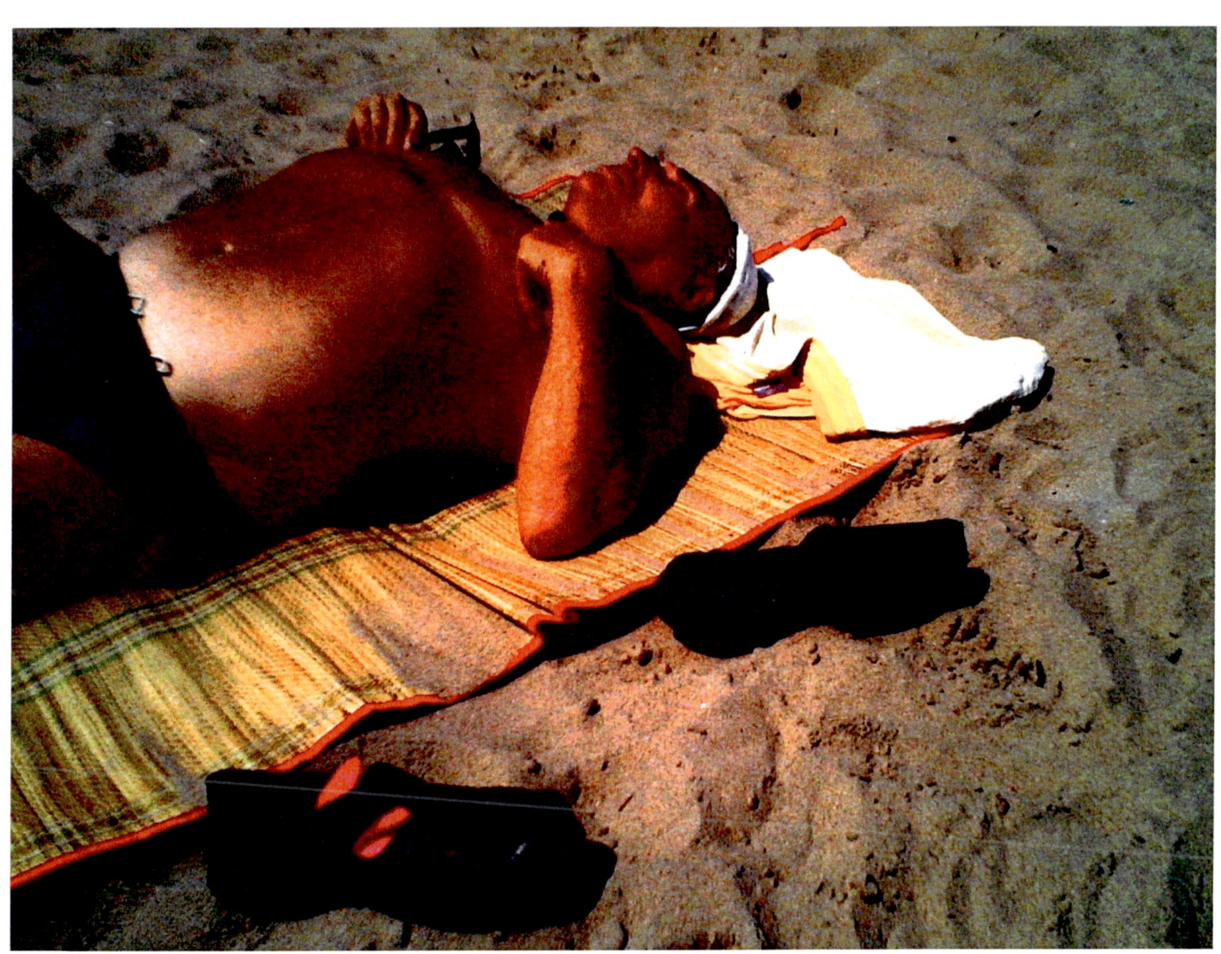

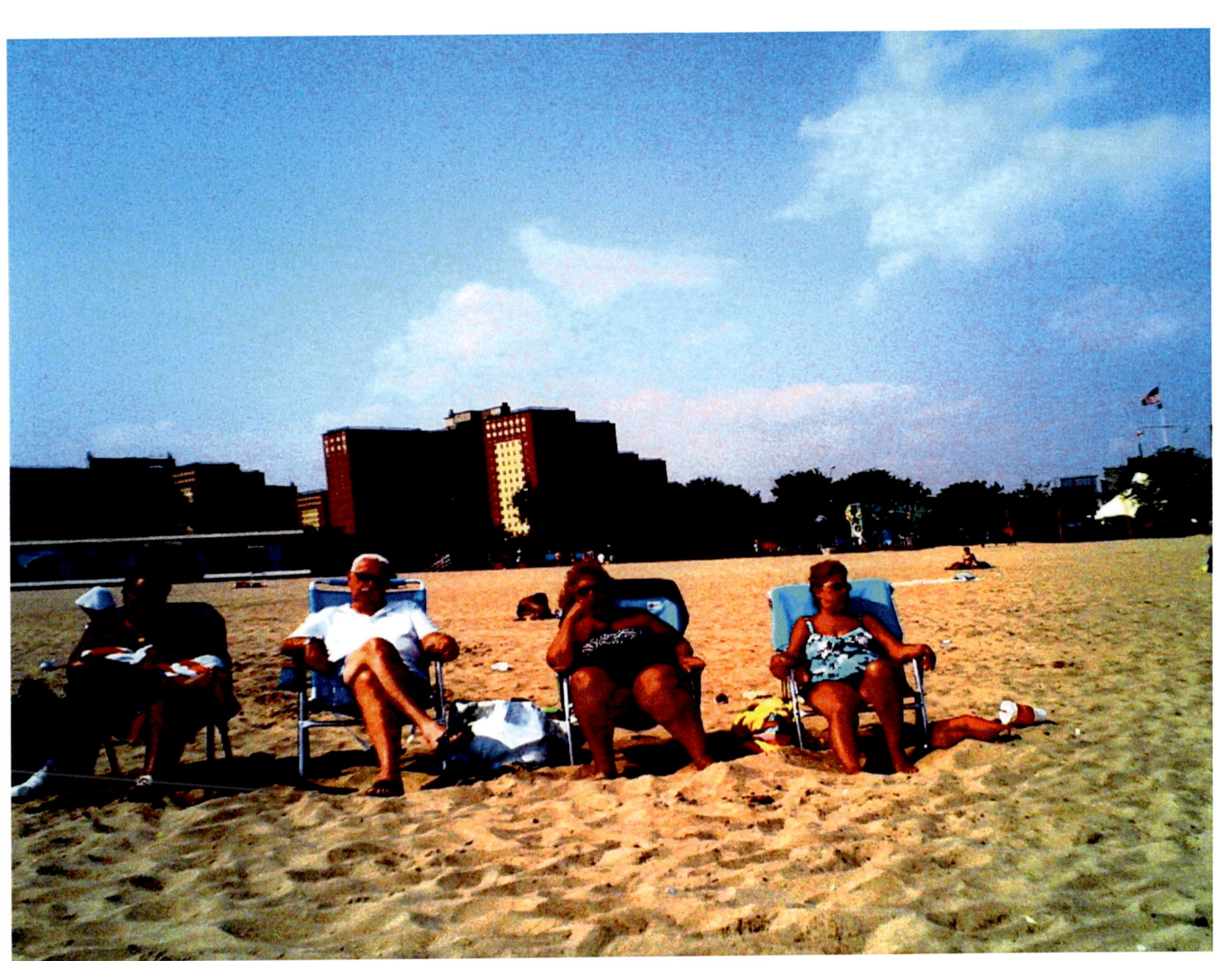

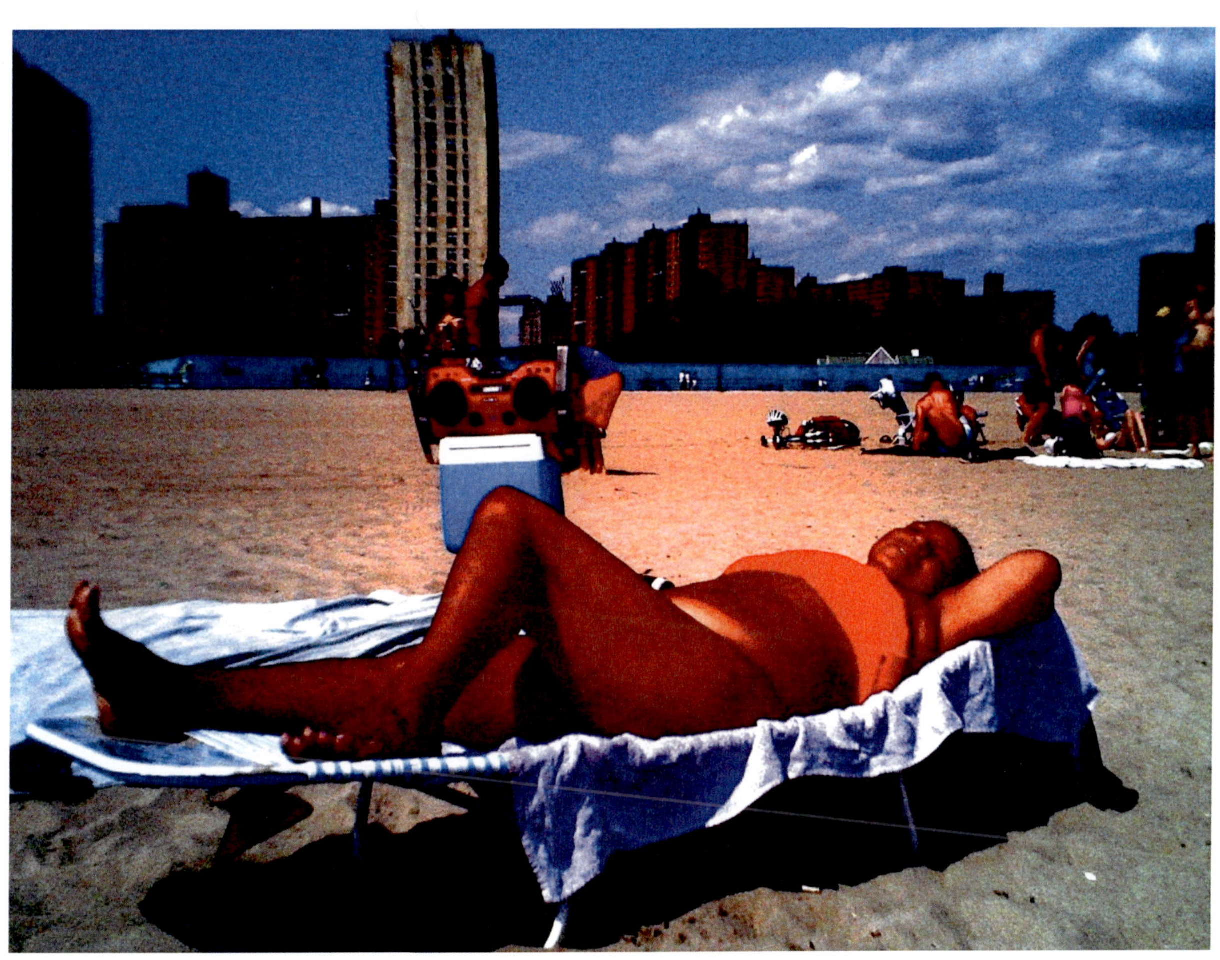

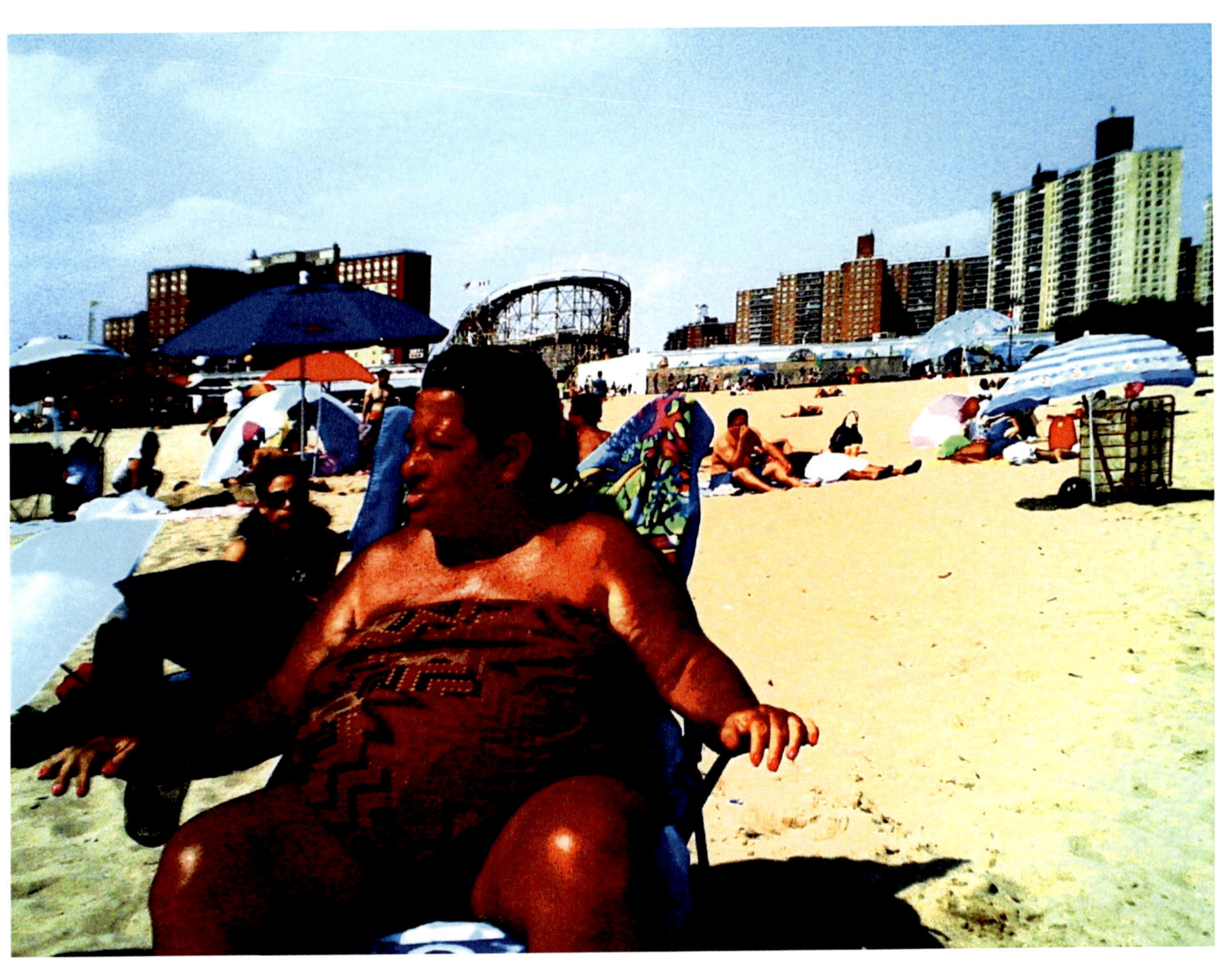

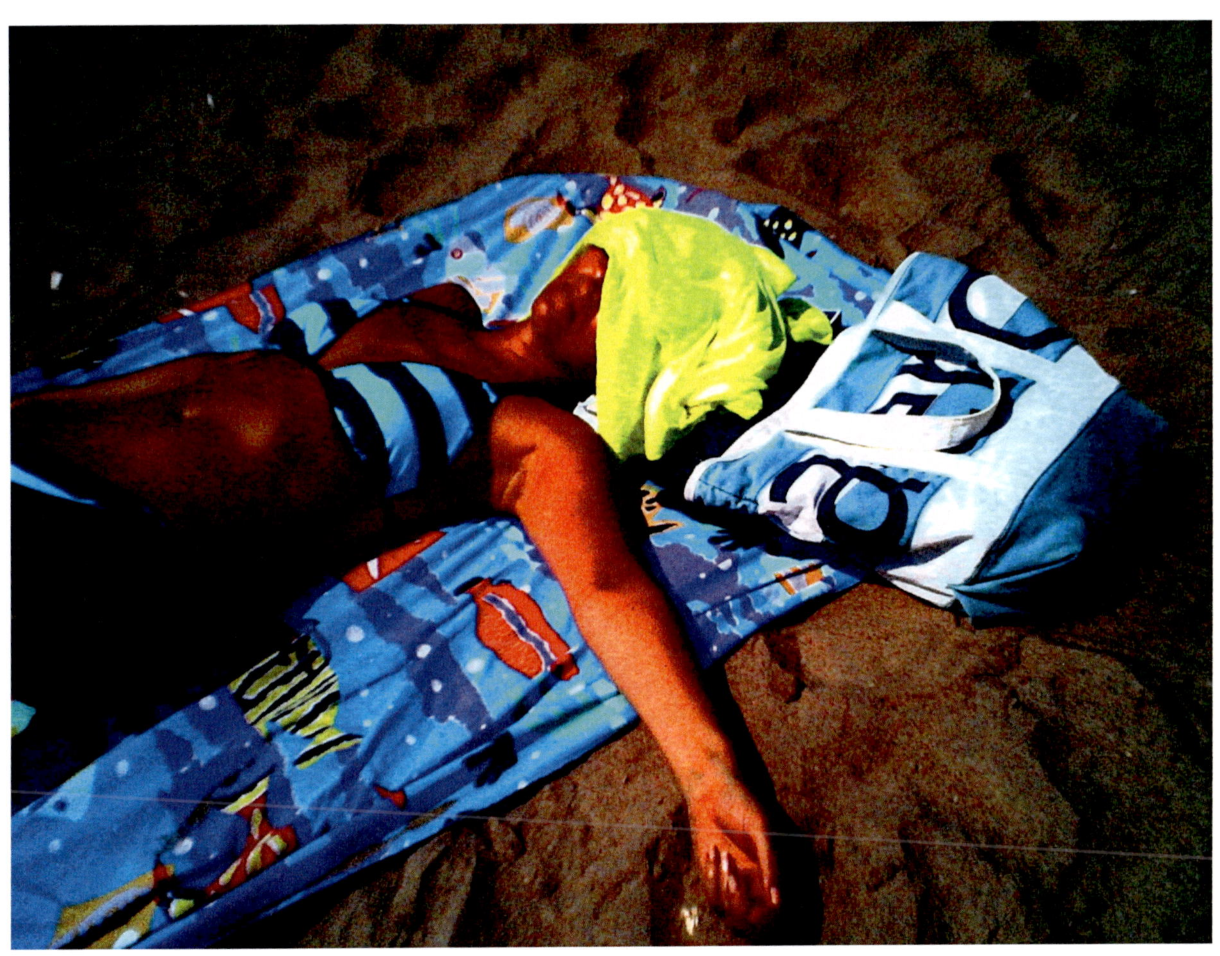

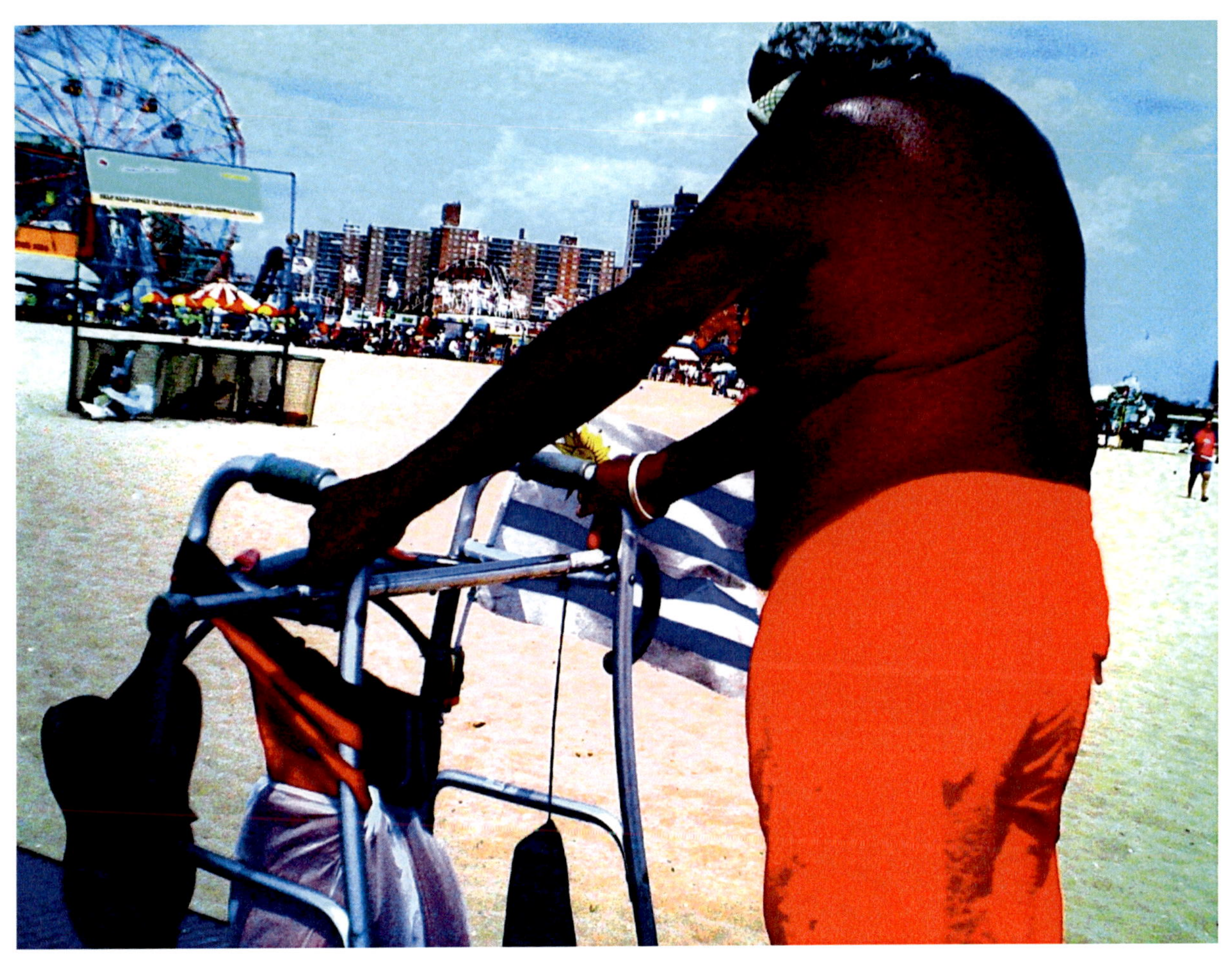

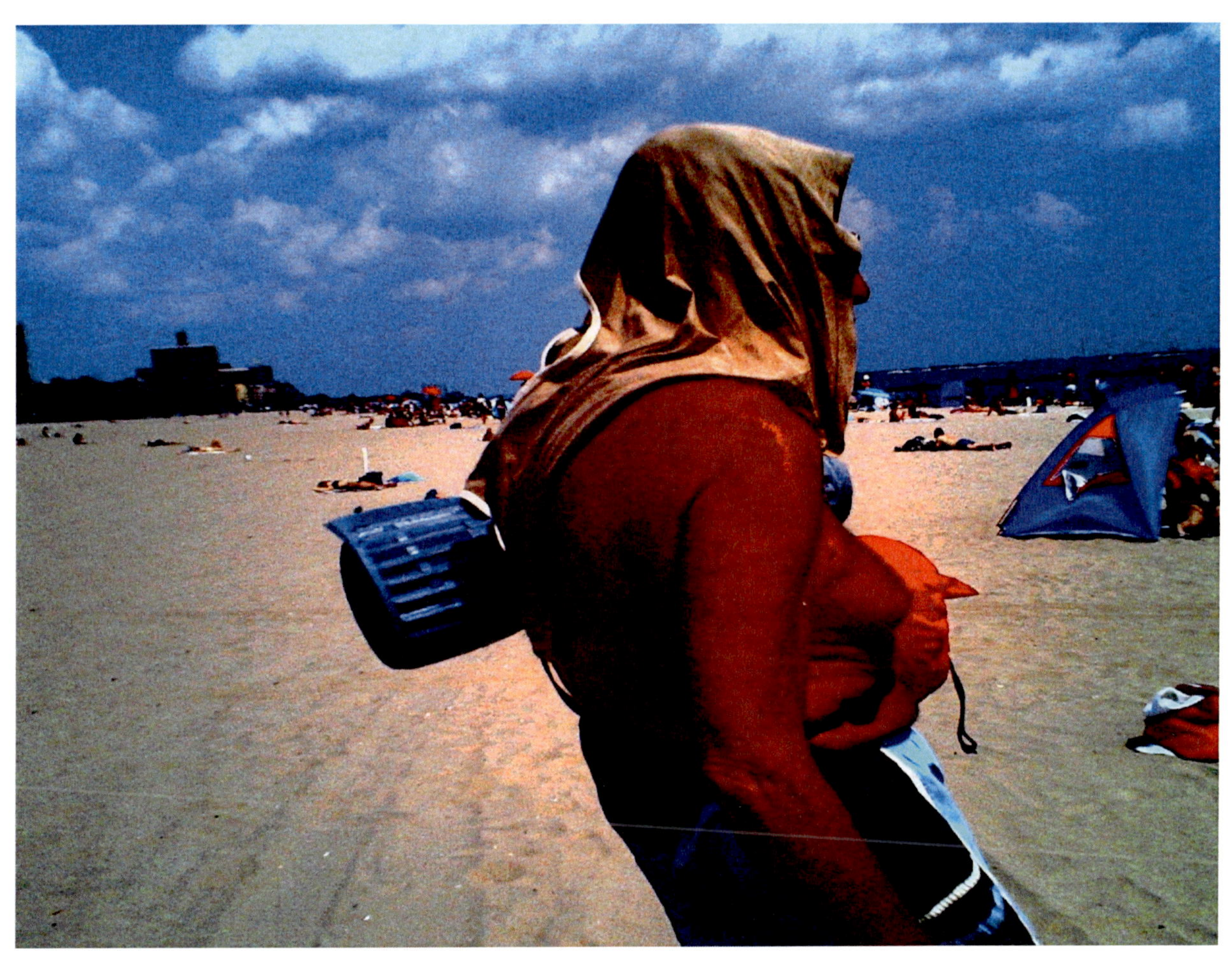

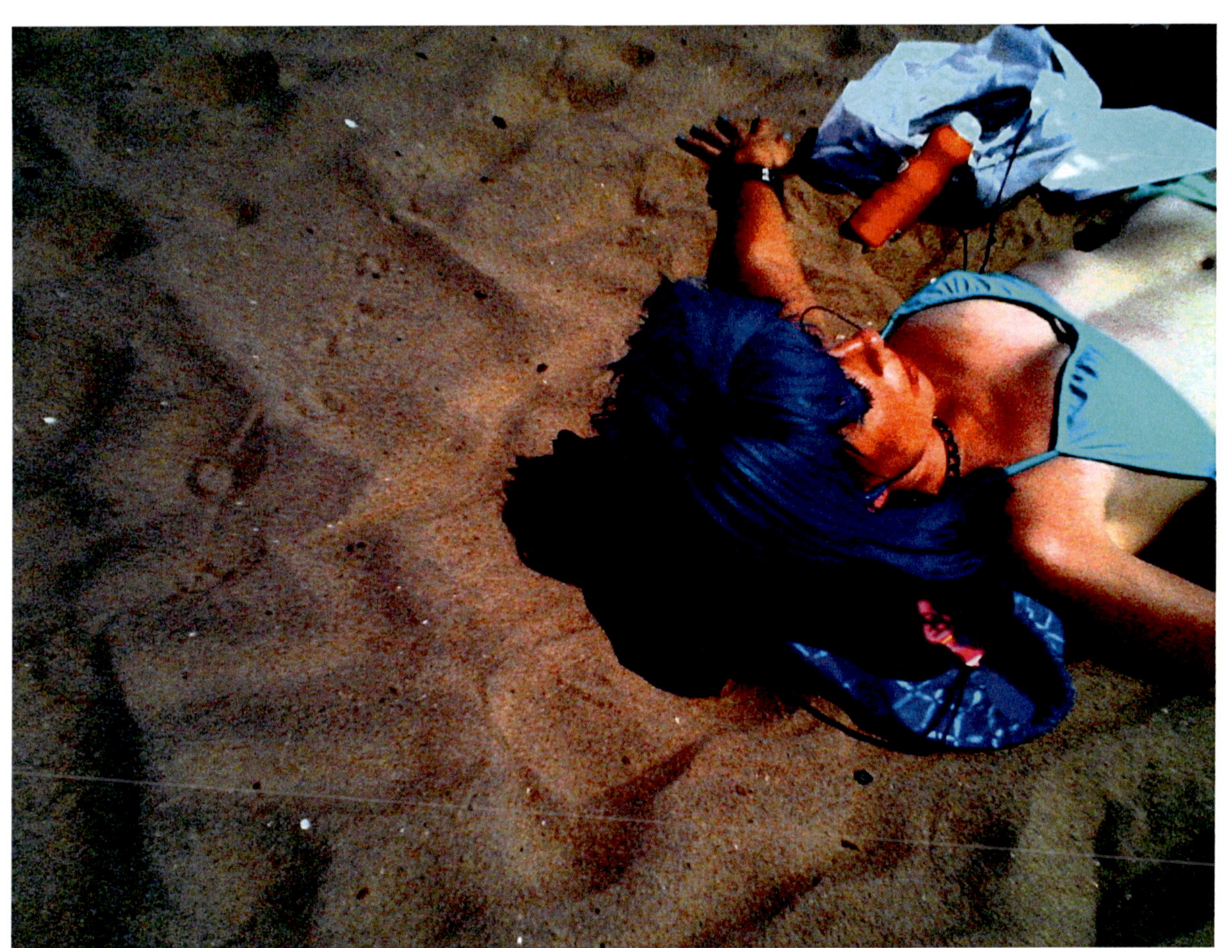

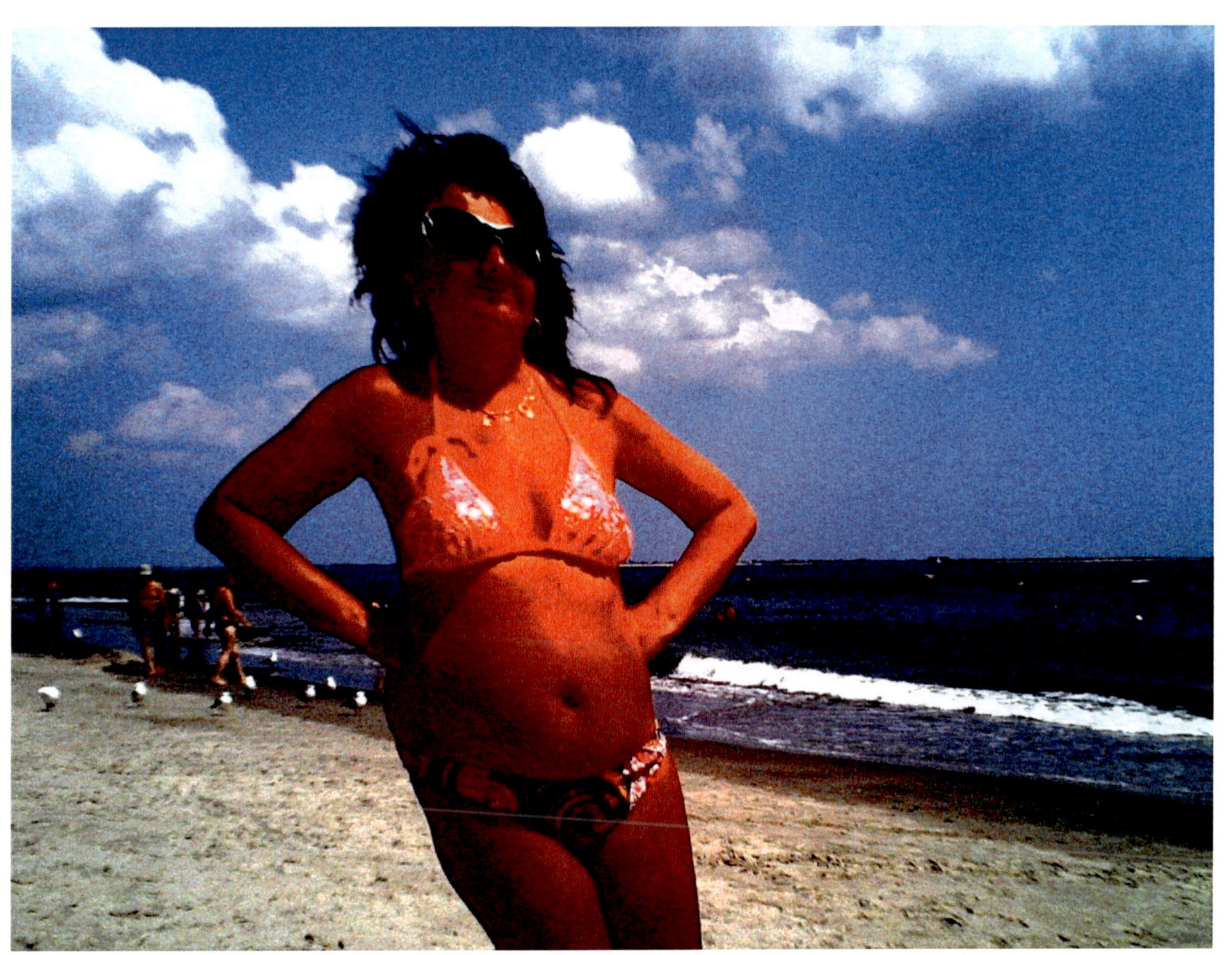

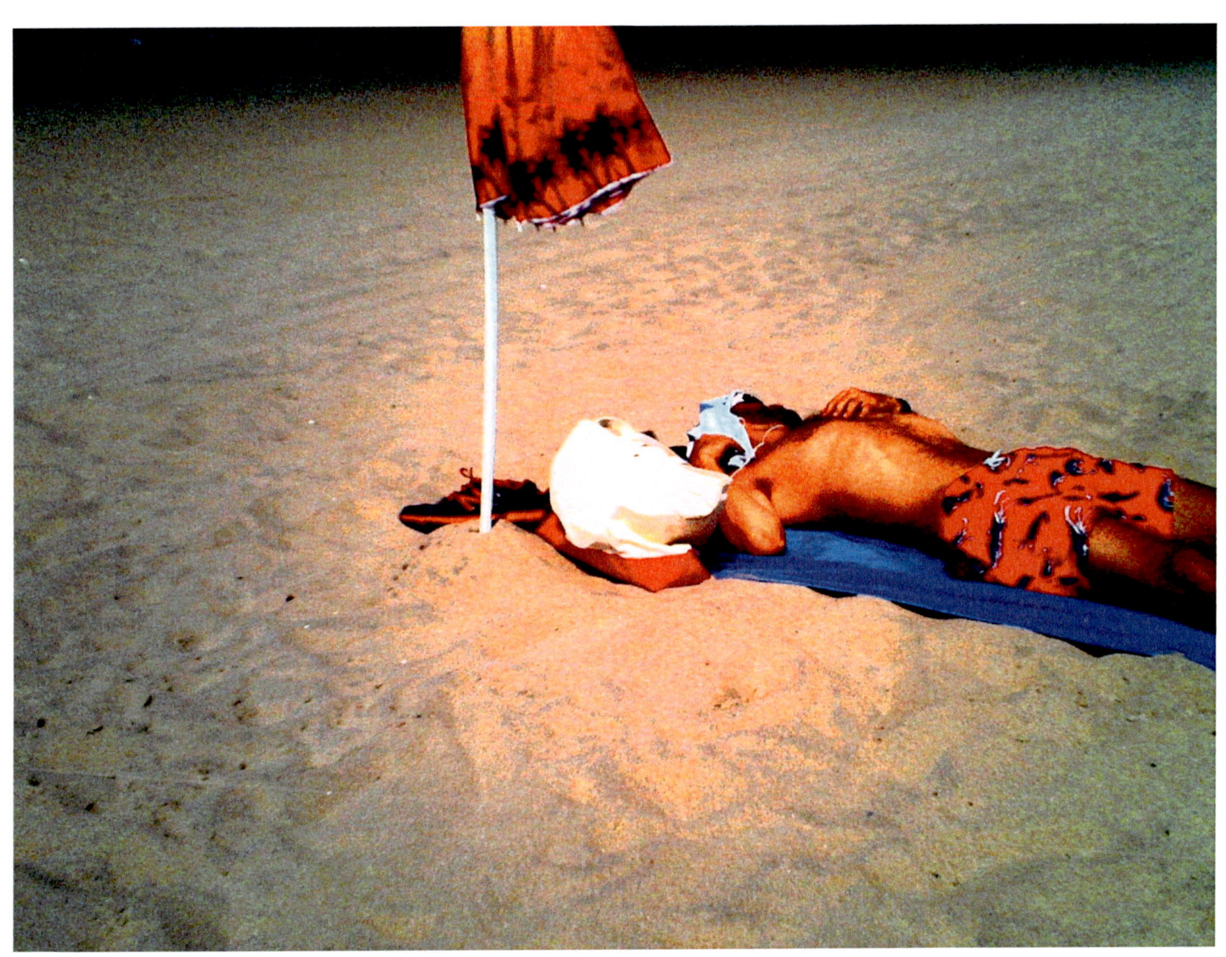

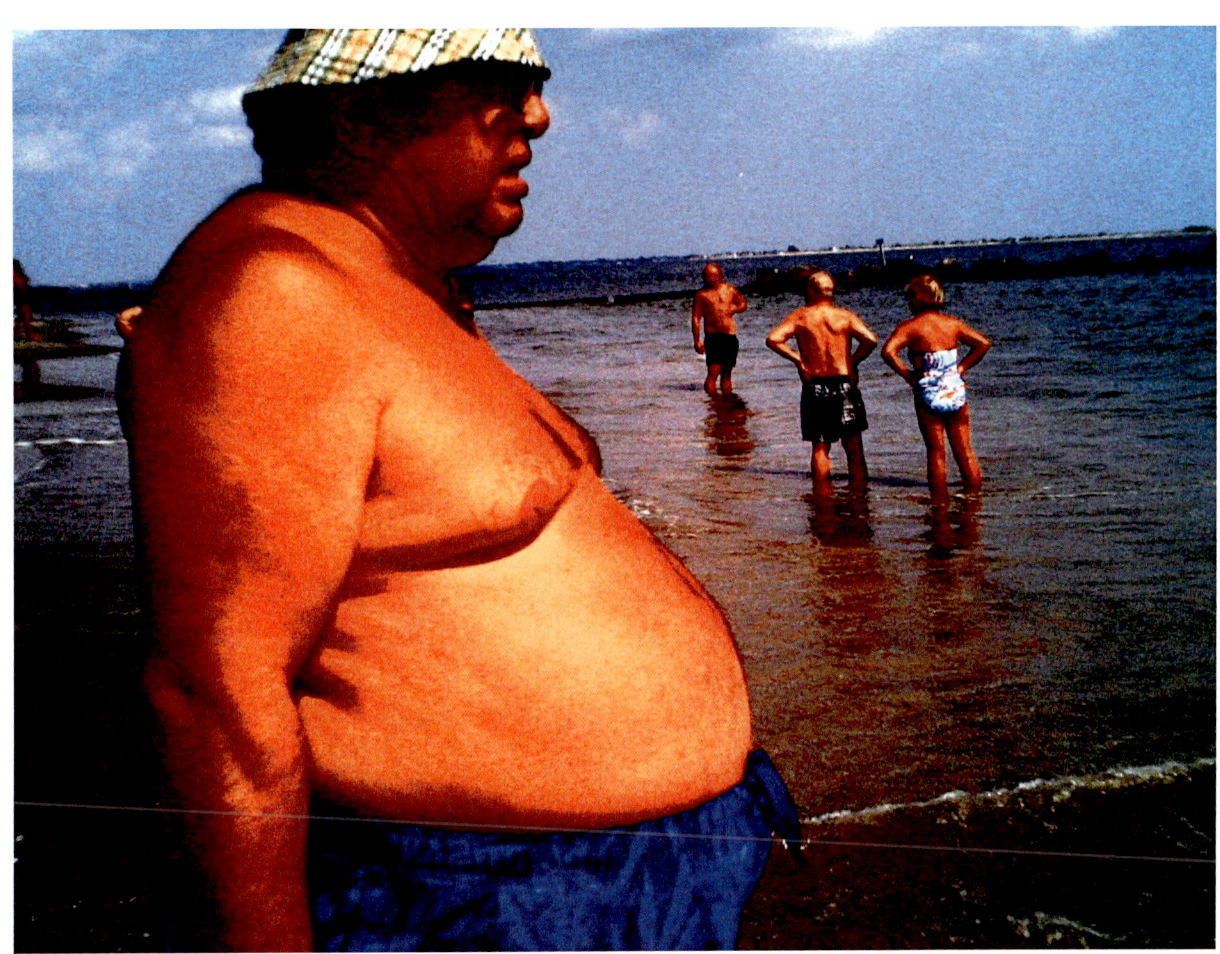

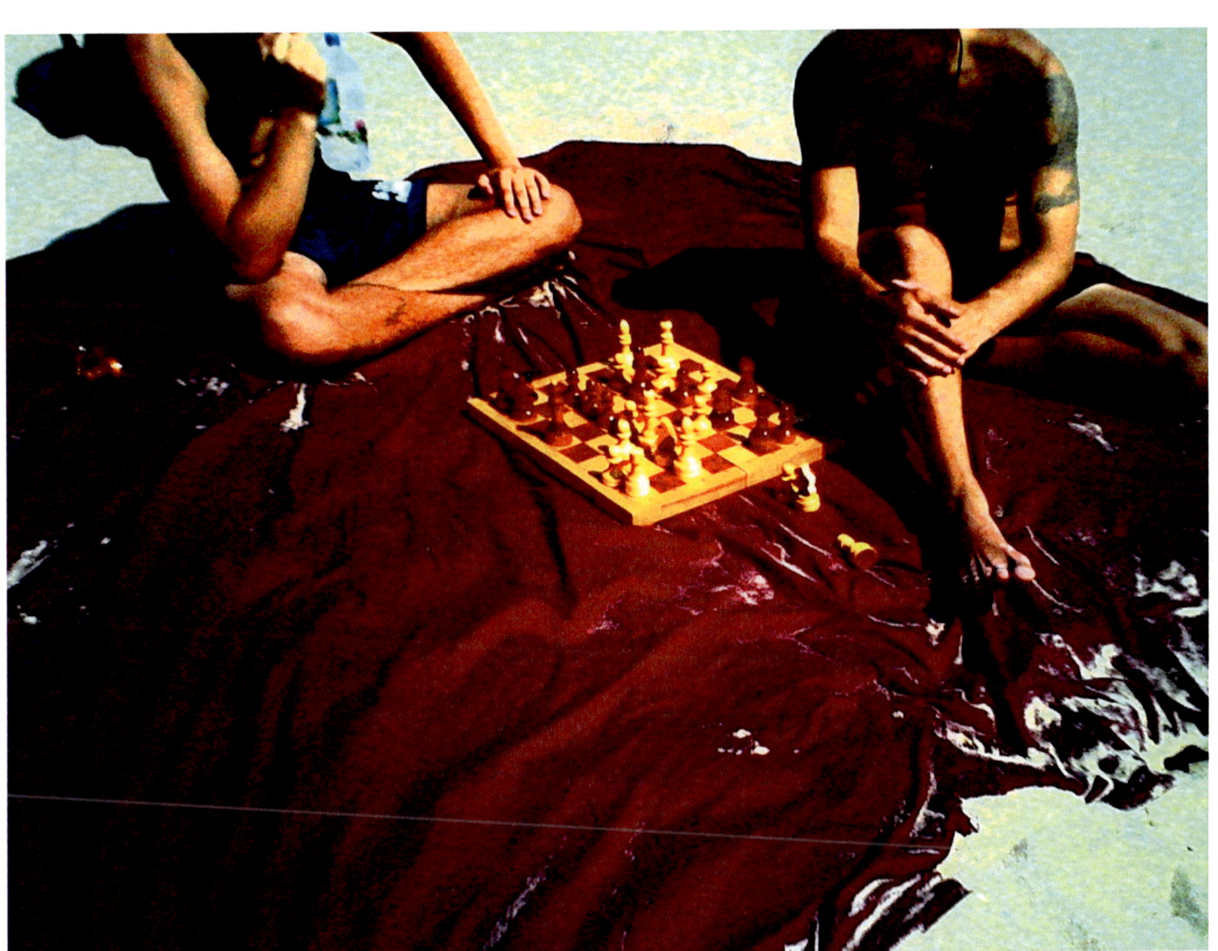

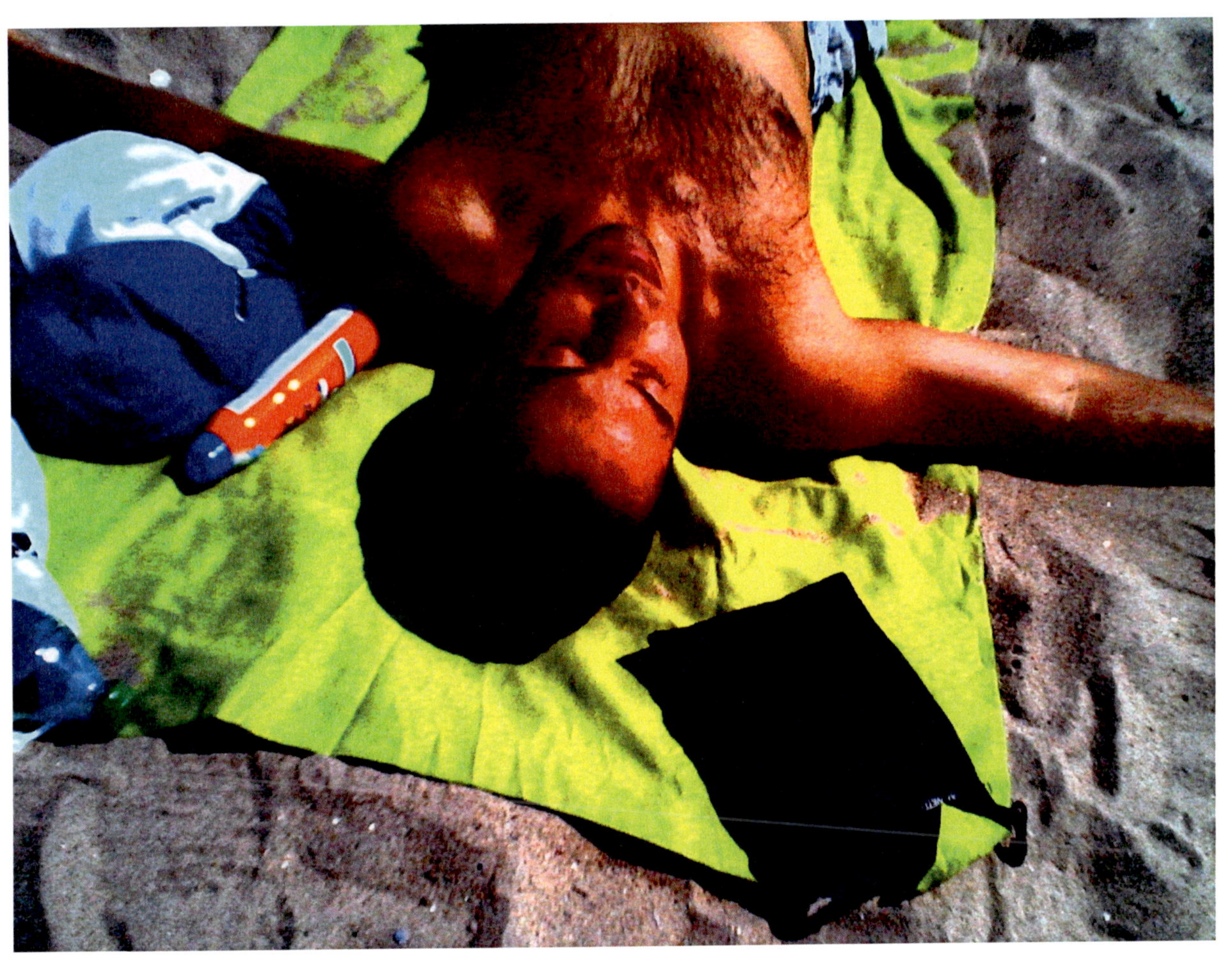

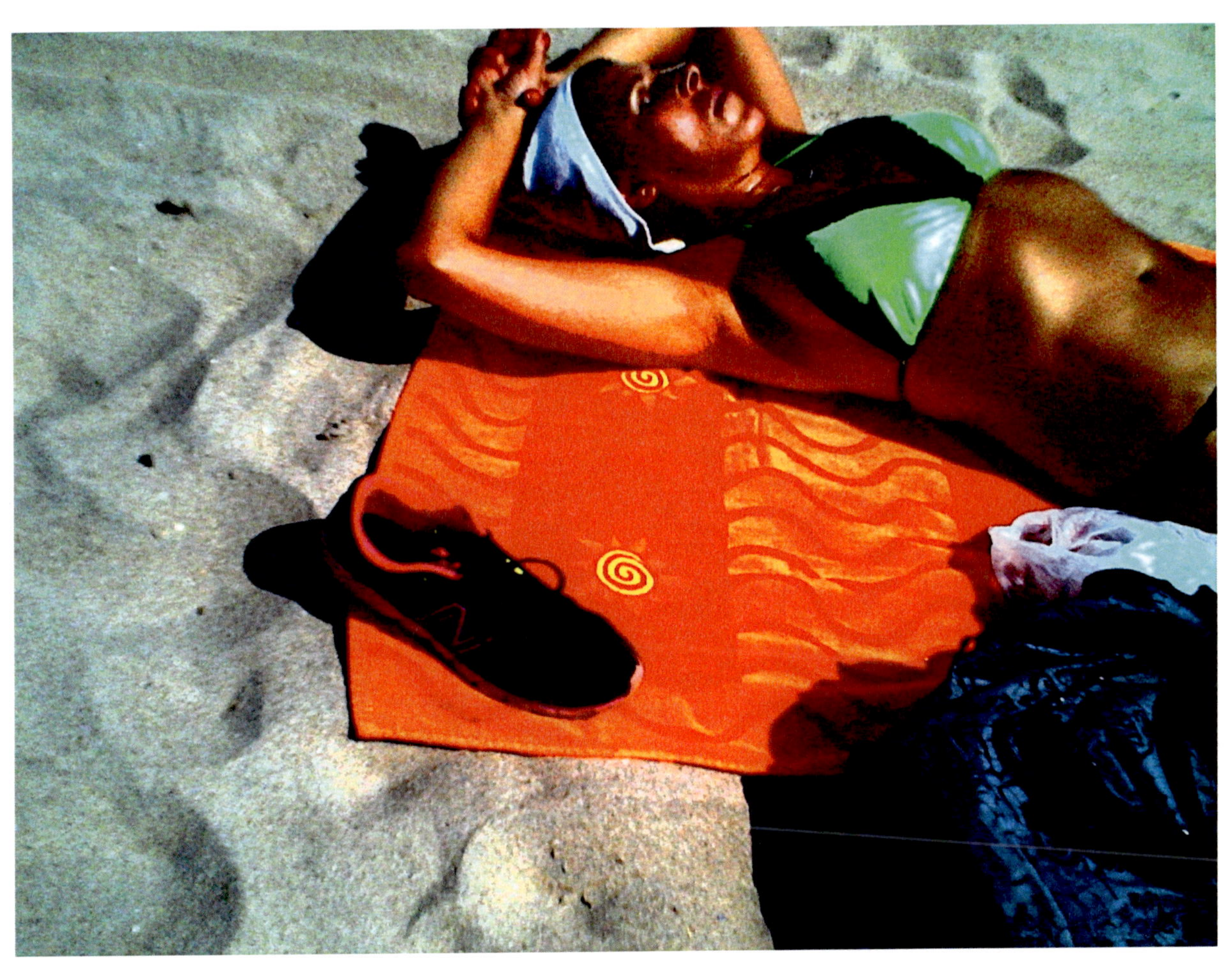

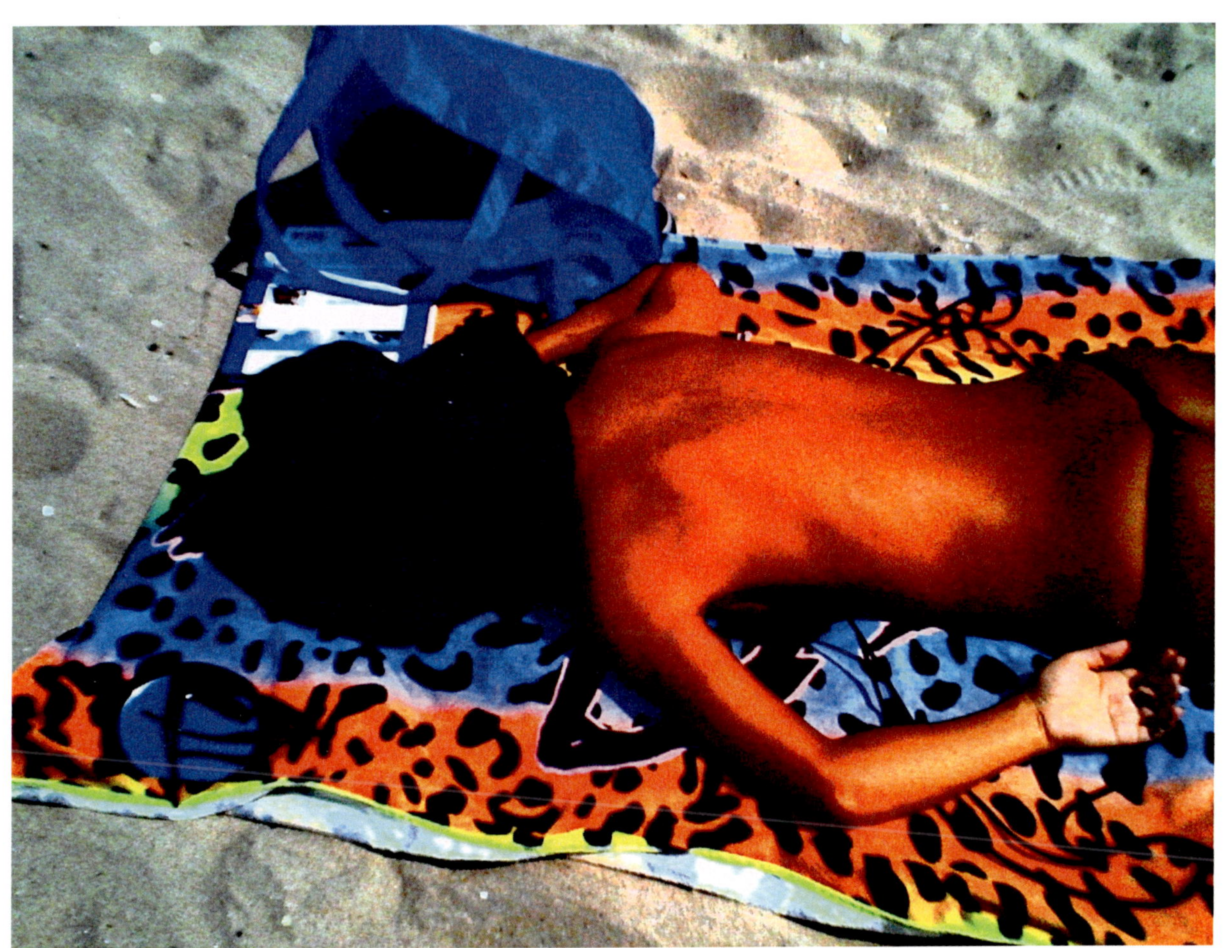

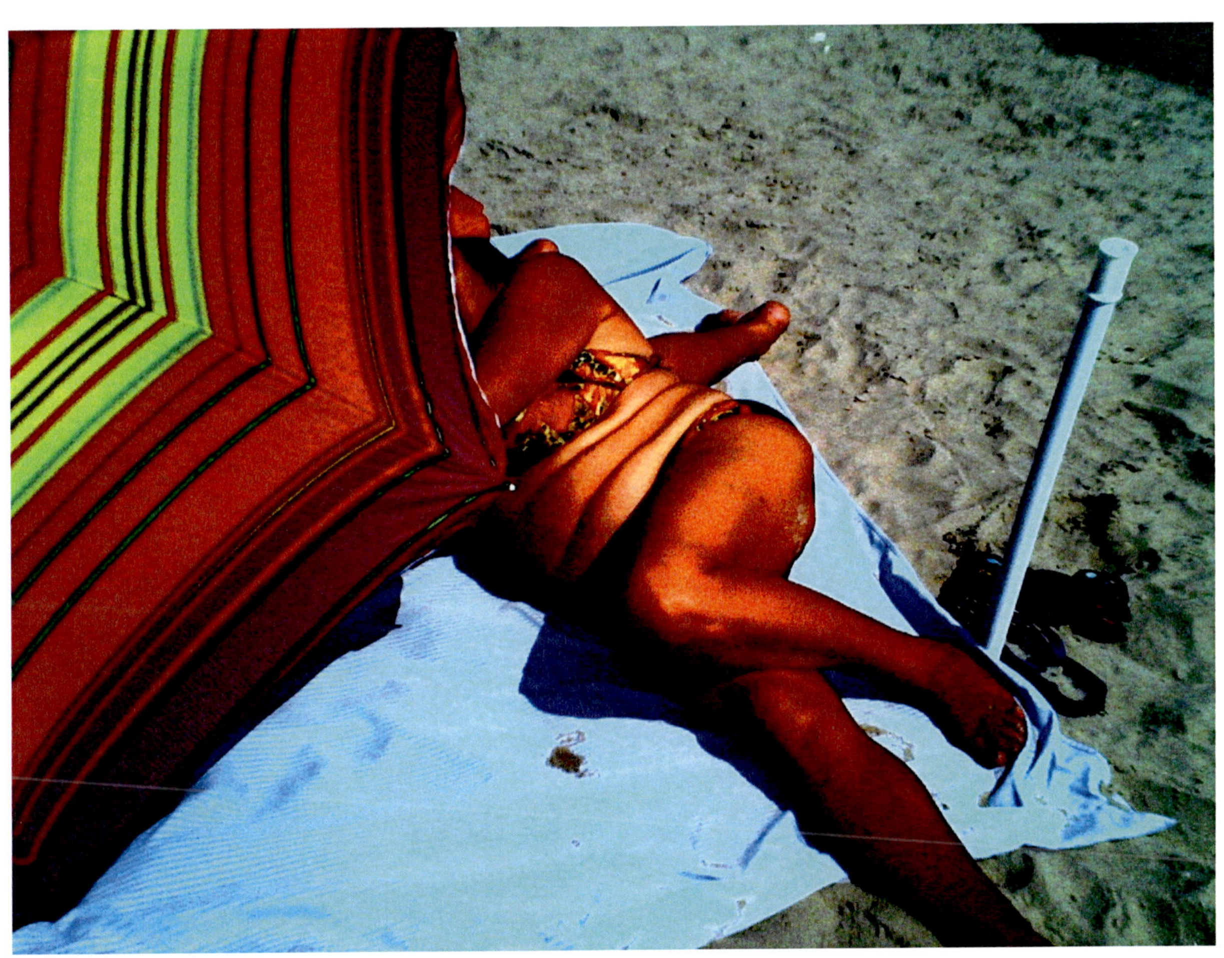

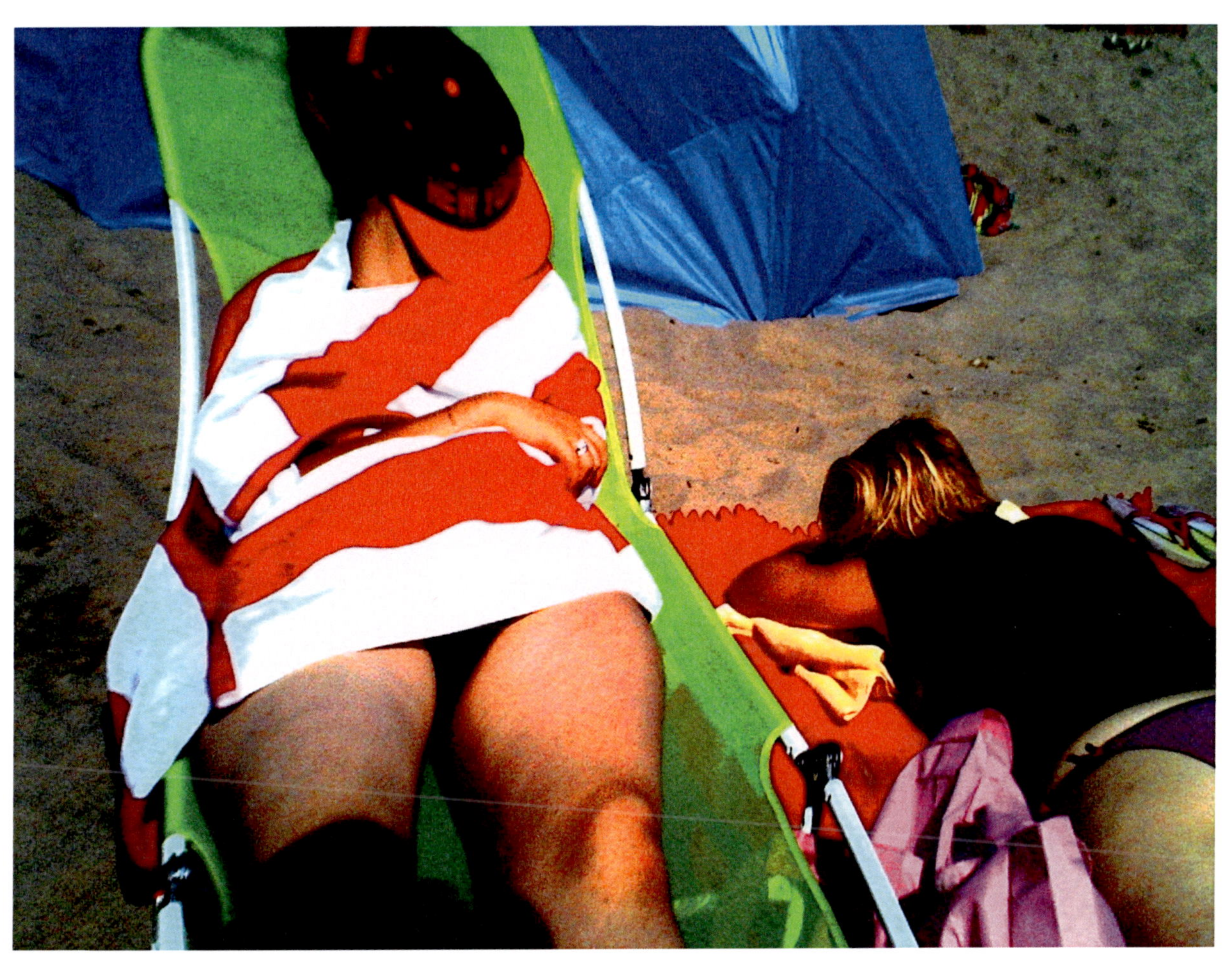

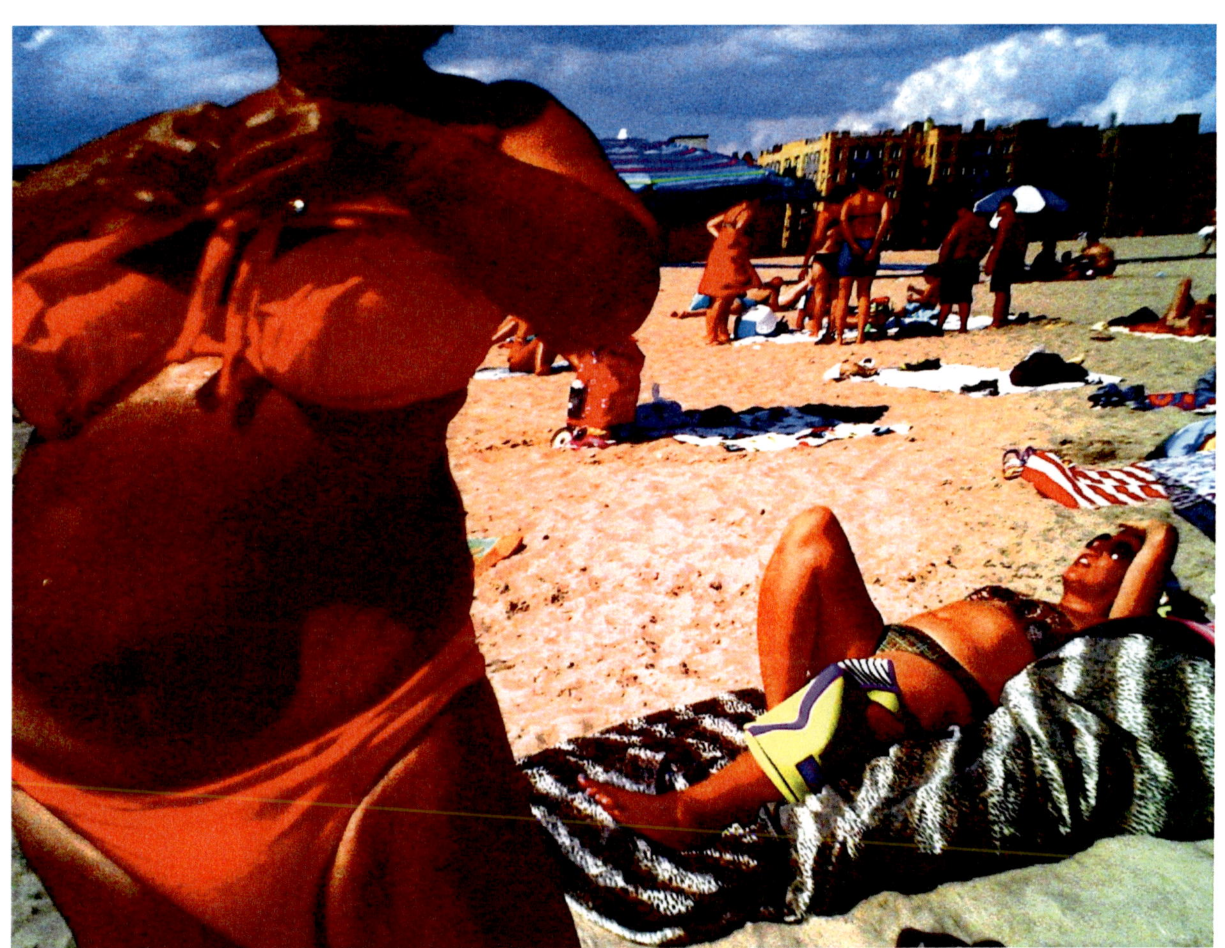

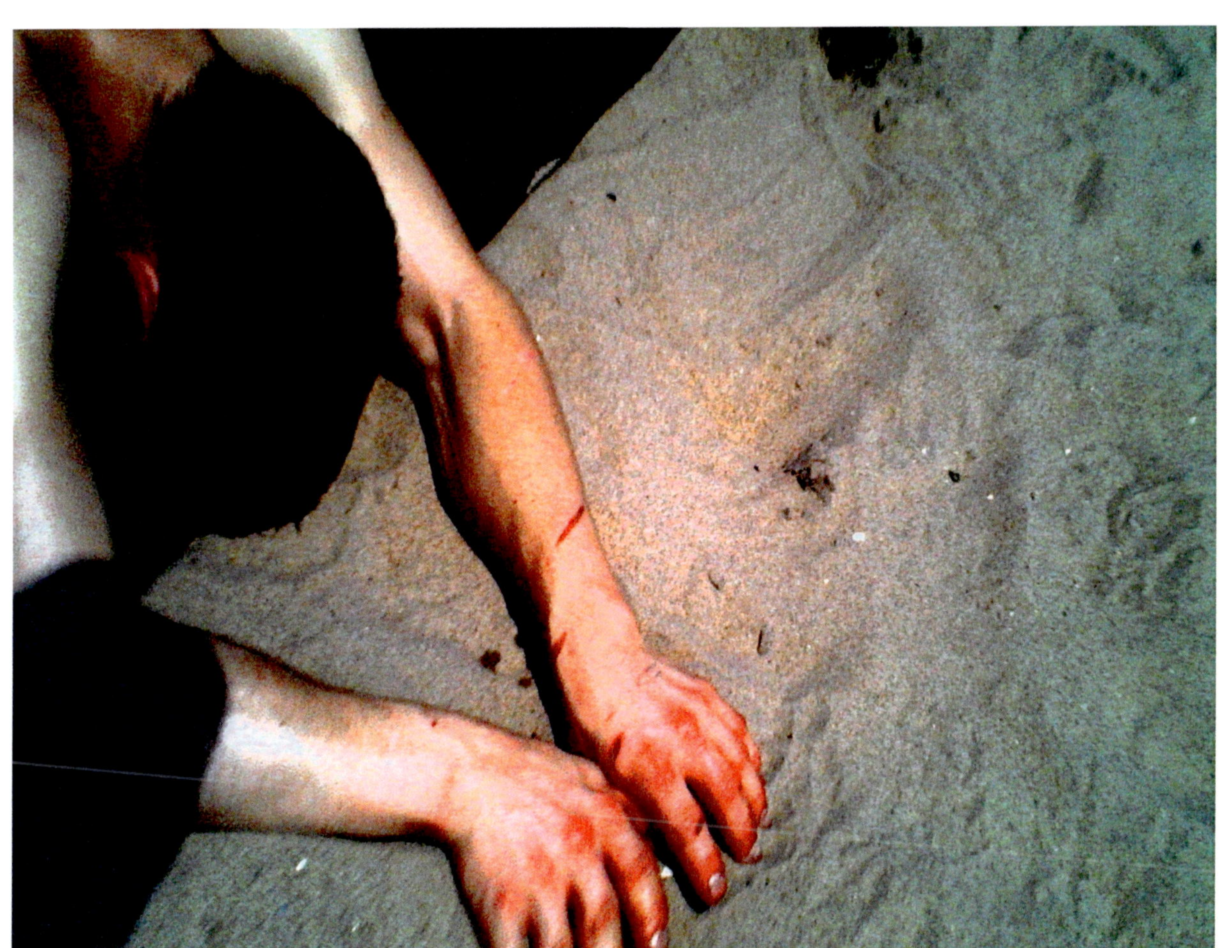

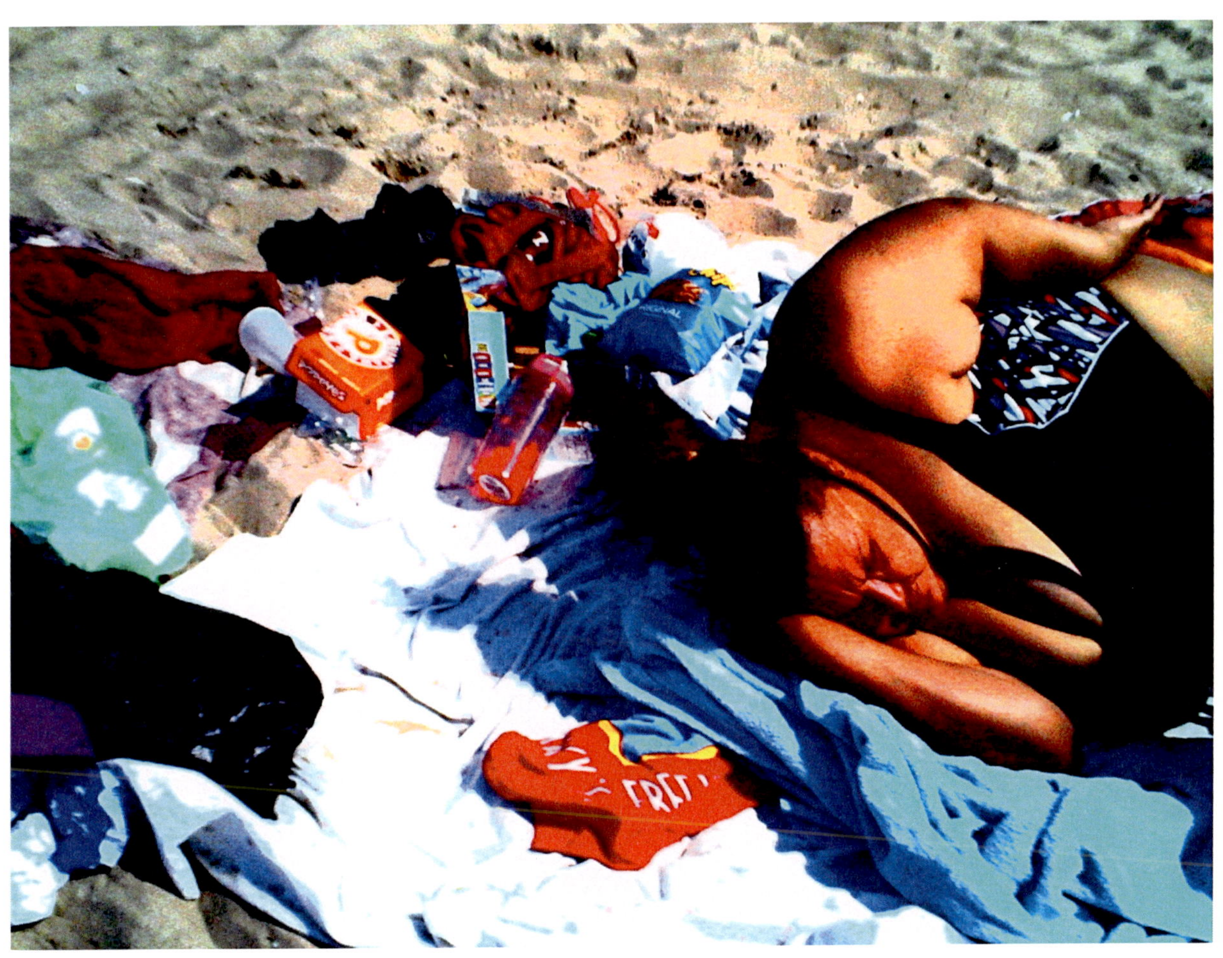

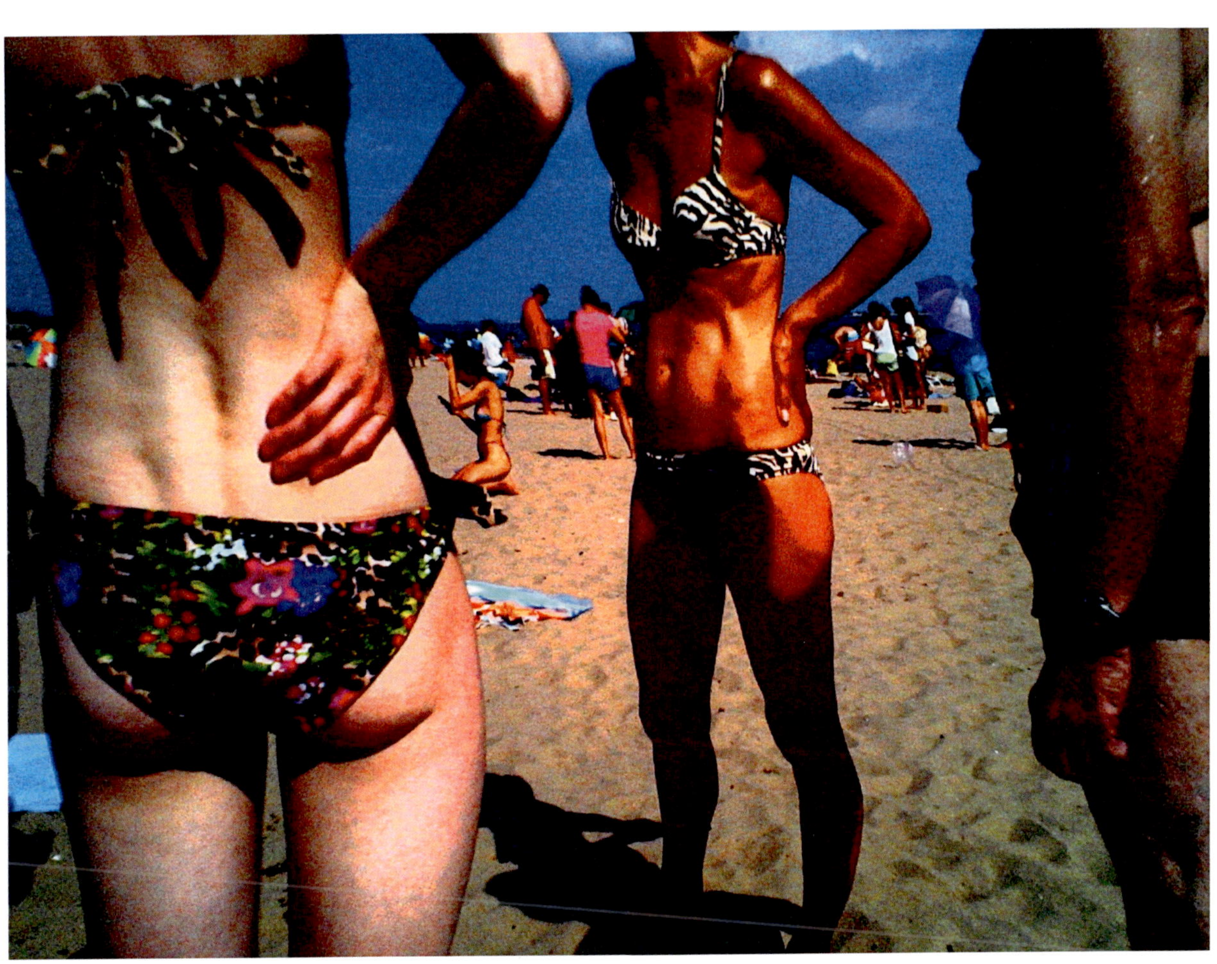

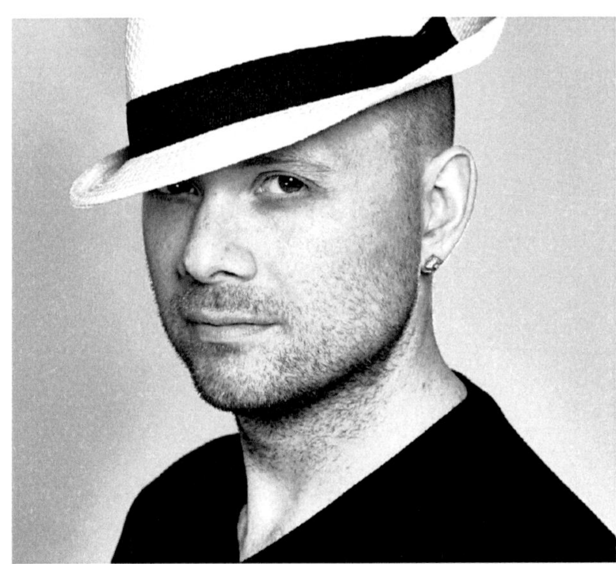
Portrait (c) Maeghan Donohue

MICHAEL ERNEST SWEET is a Canadian educator, writer, and photographer. His work has been widely published in such magazines as *Popular Photography*, *Black and White*, and *Fisheye*.

Michael is a national recipient of both a Prime Minister's Award and The Queen Elizabeth II Diamond Jubilee Medal in Canada for significant contributions to his country.

Michael's first full-length book of street photography, *The Human Fragment*, was published by Brooklyn Arts Press in 2013.

Michael divides his time between Montreal and New York City.

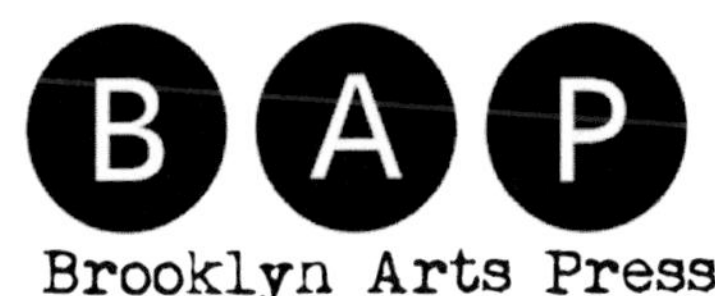

Brooklyn Arts Press

Brooklyn Arts Press, LLC
154 N 9th St #1
Brooklyn, New York 11249

www.BrooklynArtsPress.com
info@BrooklynArtsPress.com

Made in the USA
Middletown, DE
13 August 2015